Japanese Katakana for Beginners

First Steps to Mastering the Japanese Writing System

Timothy G Stout
Illustrated by Alexis Cowan

TUTTLE PUBLISHING
Toyko • Rutland, Vermont • Singapore

Published by Tuttle Publishing, an imprint of Periplus Editions (Hong Kong) Ltd., with editorial offices at 364 Innovation Drive, North Clarendon, Vermont 05759 U.S.A. and 130 Joo Seng Road #06-01, Singapore 368357.

ISBN-13: 978-4-8053-0878-3
ISBN-10: 4-8053-0878-8

Distributed by

North America, Latin America & Europe
Tuttle Publishing
364 Innovation Drive North Clarendon, VT 05759-9436 U.S.A.
Tel: 1 (802) 773-8930
Fax: 1 (802) 773-6993
info@tuttlepublishing.com
www.tuttlepublishing.com

Japan
Tuttle Publishing
Yaekari Building, 3rd Floor,
5-4-12 Osaki,
Shinagawa-ku,
Tokyo 141-0032
Tel: (81) 03 5437-0171
Fax: (81) 03 5437-0755
tuttle-sales@gol.com

Asia Pacific
Berkeley Books Pte. Ltd.
130 Joo Seng Road #06-01,
Singapore 368357
Tel: (65) 6280-1330
Fax: (65) 6280-6290
inquiries@periplus.com.sg
www.periplus.com

11 10 09 08 07   5 4 3 2 1

Printed in Singapore

Contents

Introduction

The aim of this book is to help beginning Japanese learners to quickly master katakana characters. Katakana is one of two sets of Japanese phonetic characters (used for their sounds, not their meanings). The other is hiragana. Both hiragana and katakana are essential to basic Japanese proficiency, but normally hiragana is learned first. This book is designed as a companion to *Japanese Hiragana for Beginners*. As with hiragana, you can learn to read the basic 46 katakana characters in a few hours, and with practice learn to write them in a few days.

In *Japanese Katakana for Beginners* you will find everything you need to build strong katakana skills. Helpful tips and exercises with practical example words and sentences will help you learn the characters quickly. Picture mnemonics, such as the one below, will improve your learning and recall of the katakana characters as you associate the sound and shape of a new katakana character with an already familiar word and image.

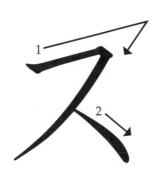

"su" as in **su**per

It's **Su**perman, er super-critter.

How to Use This Book

This book is organized into an introduction and three major sections. The introduction gives you basic information about katakana characters: where they came from, how to pronounce and write them, and how to write your name. In Section One you will learn the basic 46 katakana characters, and how to write some simple words. Section Two introduces the "rules" for making 89 more syllables—using the basic 46 katakana characters, including the special syllables for writing foreign words. Section Three provides more exercises designed not only to strengthen your newly acquired katakana skills, but also to increase your vocabulary. At the end of the book there are a set of katakana flashcards on perforated cardstock. Since it is easier to learn to read katakana than to write it, you may want to start with the katakana flashcards, and review them often while you work through Sections One, Two and Three. You will get the most out of this book by doing all of the activities. If you study for thirty minutes a day, in a few short weeks you will be a confident reader and writer of katakana.

Katakana Basics

Katakana and hiragana characters—together called **kana**, are the two sets of 46 phonetic characters used in Japanese.

- **Hiragana** is mainly used for grammatical words and original Japanese words for which there are no kanji.
- **Katakana** is mainly used to write foreign "loan words" or **gairaigo**, such as **intānetto** (the internet).

- **Kanji** or "Chinese characters" compose the majority of written Japanese: the nouns, verbs, adjectives, or "content" words. Romaji are Roman (Latin) letters used to write Japanese.

ひらがな **Hiragana**	カタカナ **Katakana**	漢字 **Kanji**	**Romaji**

You may be wondering why Japanese has "two" sets of phonetic characters. The main reason is that it makes reading easier—katakana words stand out in a text, like a highlighter. When you see a katakana word, you immediately know it falls into one of six categories:

1. **Gairaigo** or "loan words"
2. Foreign place names and personal names
3. Onomatopoeia (sound symbolic words), like "buzz," "flip" and "bow wow," which are much more numerous in Japanese than in English
4. Emphasis words—normally written in hiragana or kanji, but that the writer wants to draw attention to
5. Dictionaries entries of **on-yomi** or the "Chinese readings" of kanji
6. Others, such as telegrams, transcriptions of the Ainu language (indigenous to northern Japan), and some official documents of pre-modern Japan

Gairaigo or "loan words," such as **konpyūtā** (computer), **nyūsu** (news), and **resutoran** (restaurant), comprise the biggest category of katakana words, with tens of thousands in common use. Most **gairaigo** come from English, so even beginning learners can often correctly guess what a Japanese article is about just from scanning the text for **gairaigo**. Topics like sports, medicine, business, economy, technology, and science have numerous **gairaigo**.

Historically, katakana and hiragana characters were developed for very different purposes. Katakana characters were developed by Buddhist priests in the 9th century as pronunciation aids for ambiguous and difficult to read official and religious texts. Katakana means "parts of kana" or parts of the **manyo-gana** characters originally used to write Japanese. Hiragana characters were developed during this same period, but for the purpose of writing personal texts, such as diaries, letters and works of fiction. Hiragana characters were based on simplified versions of whole **manyo-gana** characters.

At first, katakana may seem to be as formidable as an opponent in martial arts, but if you stick at it, you will be the master, "I know katakana and I'm not afraid to use it. Hai ya!"

How to Pronounce Katakana

Katakana and hiragana are pronounced the same way. The first five characters are the five Japanese vowels. Japanese vowels are short and clipped compared to English vowels. (All of the examples in this book use Standard American English pronunciation).

a	as in father
i	as in easy
u	as in you
e	as in red
o	as in oak

The rest of the katakana characters are consonant-vowel combinations, with the consonant always coming first (e.g., "ka," "ki," "ku," "ke" and "ko"). The one exception is the single consonant syllable "n" that is pronounced by touching the back of the tongue to the roof of the mouth, as in "ink" and "sing." Many Japanese consonants are commonly found in English and are easy to pronounce.

k	as in coat		g	as in goat (voiced version of k)
s	as in Sue		z	as in zoo (voiced version of g)
t	as in tie		d	as in dye (voiced version of t)
n	as in no			
h	as in house			
p	as in pig		b	as in big (voiced version of p)
m	as in man			

Several Japanese consonants, however, are not commonly found in English and require special attention. One is the Japanese "r." In English "r" is pronounced by curling the tongue so the sides touch the upper teeth (not touching the tip of the tongue). In Japanese, "r" is pronounced by tapping the tongue against the ridge behind the upper teeth, as in "paddle" and "ladder," sounding like a combination of "l" and "d"; it is not a rolling trill as in Spanish. "tsu" is pronounced as in "tsunami" and "cat's whiskers." "fu" is pronounced without touching the upper teeth and lower lip. It almost sounds like "who" and "hooting owl," except the lips are more pursed and air escapes more quickly.

The special consonant "y" as in "yarn" is paired with the vowels "a," "u" and "o" to make the syllables "ya," "yu" and "yo." This consonant is special because Japanese uses it extensively in combination with all of the other consonants to form additional syllables, such as "kya," "kyu" and "kyo." In order to accommodate more foreign syllables, many more character combinations are used in katakana (see Section Two).

Although katakana tries to represent **gairaigo** as faithfully as possible, the words sound distinctly Japanese. In 1991 the Japanese government updated the official guidelines for writing **gairaigo**. The guidelines included 33 more combined characters for writing foreign words. These 33 combined characters are not the limit—the guidelines clearly state that other combinations can be made as needed. Still, all syllables must conform to the basics of Japanese phonology (see Section Two).

How to Write Katakana

Katakana characters are composed of three types of strokes: "stops," "jumps" and "brushes." With a stop, the pencil must come to a stop before it is removed from the paper. Jumps are written by removing the pencil from the paper as it moves to the next stroke. With a brush, the pencil is slowly removed from the paper as the stroke is written, giving it a tapered, sweeping appearance. In the following example, the character "o" as in "oak" is written with all three types of strokes. The first is a stop, the second a jump, and the third is a brush.

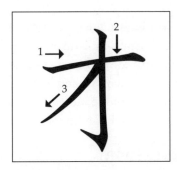

Compare the hiragana and katakana characters below. Hiragana characters are curved and looping, but katakana characters are straight and angled. Katakana also has fewer "jumps" and more "stops" and "brushes."

a	i	ka	ki	sa	shi	ta	chi
あ	い	か	き	さ	し	た	ち
ア	イ	カ	キ	サ	シ	タ	チ

Some hiragana and katakana characters look alike, like "ka" and "ki." The picture mnemonics for these katakana characters are the same as the hiragana characters—another good reason you should master *Japanese Hiragana for Beginners* first.

Writing the correct stroke type in the correct order is important for forming balanced, legible characters. With practice you will get the hang of it. You can make your characters look more authentic by slightly tilting left-to-right strokes, as in stroke one in "o" (see above), rather than writing them straight across. Character strokes are generally written from left to right and top to bottom. Try to center each character in the middle of an imaginary box, not too far to the top, bottom, left, or right.

オ	オ	オ	オ	オ
Correct!	**Wrong**	**Wrong**	**Wrong**	**Wrong**

Writing Your Name in Japanese

Try to find your name in the following lists. The list is based on the Social Security Administration list published in 1998 (www.socialsecurity.gov/OACT/babynames Viewed 8/2/2006). Only one Japanese spelling is given for all of the names with the same pronunciation, such as Amy, Ami, Amie and Aimee. The names are listed under the most common spelling. If you don't see your name in the list and your name is a nickname, try looking for the formal version (i.e., "Richard" instead of "Rick"). If you still can't find your name, it may not be one of the top 300 most common girls' and boys' names. Never fear, you can ask your teacher or a Japanese friend for help. Any name can be written in Japanese. Practice writing your name in the spaces provided (don't worry if you leave some boxes unused).

Most beginning learners enjoy katakana because it is relatively simple to learn, and it is immediately useful. You write your name and your friends' names in katakana. You can guess many of the katakana words found in Japanese texts you read. Soon reading and writing katakana will become second nature, and all your hard work will begin to pay off. Remember that step by step is possible, and *Japanese Katakana for Beginners* is designed to help you master this important step of Japanese proficiency. Good luck, as you continue on your journey, and with all of the opportunities that will open up for you!

300 Most Common Girls' Names (1998)

Aleah アリーヤ	Avery エイヴァリー	Courtney コートニー
Abby アビー	Ayanna アヤナ	Crystal クリスタル
Abigail アビゲール	Bailey ベイリー	Cynthia シンシア
Adriana エイドリアナ	Bethany ベサニー	Daisy デイジー
Adrienne エイドリエン	Bianca ビアンカ	Dakota ダコタ
Aileen アイリーン	Brandi ブランディ	Dana デイナ
Aisha アイーシャ	Brenda ブレンダ	Daniela ダニエラ
Alana アラーナ	Brenna ブレナ	Danielle ダニエール
Alejandra アレハンドラ	Brianna ブリアナ	Deanna ディアナ
Alexa アレクサ	Brianne ブリアーン	Deja ディア
Alexandra アレクサンドラ	Bridget ブリジット	Delaney ディレイニ
Alexandria アレクサンドリア	Brooke ブルック	Denise デニース
Alexia アレクシア	Brooklyn ブルックリン	Desiree デザリー
Alexis アレクシス	Callie カリー	Destiny デスティニー
Alicia アリシア	Cameron キャメロン	Devin デヴィン
Allie アリー	Camille カミール	Diamond ダイアモンド
Allison アリソン	Candace キャンディス	Diana ダイアナ
Alondra アロンドラ	Carissa カリッサ	Dominique ドミニク
Alyssa アリッサ	Carly カーリー	Elena エレーナ
Amanda アマンダ	Carmen カーメン	Elise エリーズ
Amber アンバー	Carolina キャロライナ	Elizabeth エリザベス
Amelia アメリア	Caroline キャロライン	Emily エミリー
Amy エイミー	Carolyn キャロリン	Emma エマ
Anastasia アナスタシア	Carrie キャリー	Erica エリカ
Andrea アンドリア	Casey ケイシー	Erin エリン
Angel エンジェル	Cassandra カサンドラ	Esmeralda エスメラルダ
Angela アンジェラ	Cassidy キャシディー	Esther エスター
Angelica アンジェリカ	Cassie キャシー	Eva エヴァ
Angelina アンジェリーナ	Cecilia セシリア	Evelyn エヴァリン
Anna アナ	Celeste セレスト	Faith フェイス
Anne アン	Charlotte シャーロット	Francesca フランシスカ
April エイプリル	Chelsey チェルシー	Gabriela ガブリエラ
Ariana エリアナ	Cheyenne シャイアン	Gabrielle ガブリエル
Ariel アリエル	Chloe クロエ	Genesis ジェネシス
Ashley アシュリー	Christina クリスティーナ	Gianna ジアナ
Ashlyn アシュリン	Christine クリスティーン	Gina ジーナ
Ashton アシュトン	Christy クリスティ	Giselle ジゼル
Asia アジア	Cindy シンディ	Grace グレース
Aubrey オーブリー	Claire クレア	Guadalupe グアダルーペ
Audrey オードリー	Clarissa クラリッサ	Haley ヘイリー
Autumn オータム	Claudia クローディア	Hallie ハリー

Hannah ハナ
Harley ハーリー
Heather ヘザー
Heidi ハイディ
Holly ホリー
Hope ホープ
Hunter ハンター
Imani イマニ
Isabel イザベル
Isabella イザベラ
Jacey ジェイシー
Jacqueline ジャクリーン
Jada ジェイダ
Jade ジェイド
Jaelyn ジェイリン
Jailene ジェイリーン
Jamie ジェイミー
Janae ジェネイ
Janelle ジャネル
Jasmine ジャスミン
Jenna ジェナ
Jennifer ジェニファー
Jenny ジェニー
Jessica ジェシカ
Jessie ジェシー
Jillian ジリアン
Joanna ジョアナ
Jocelyn ジョスリン
Jordan ジョーダン
Julia ジュリア
Julianna ジュリアナ
Julie ジュリー
Julissa ジュリッサ
Kaitlyn ケイトリン
Kara キャラ
Karen カレン
Karina カリーナ
Karla カーラ
Kate ケイト
Katherine キャサリン
Kathleen キャスリーン
Katie ケイティ
Katrina カトリーナ
Kayla ケイラ
Kaylee ケイリー
Kaylin ケイリン
Kelly ケリー
Kelsey ケルシー
Kendall ケンダル

Kendra ケンドラ
Kennedy ケネディ
Kiana キアナ
Kiara キアラ
Kimberly キンバリー
Kirsten カーステン
Krista クリスタ
Kristen クリステン
Kyla カイラ
Kylie カイリー
Kyra カイラ
Lacey レイシー
Laura ローラ
Lauren ローレン
Leah リア
Leann リアン
Leslie レスリー
Lexi レクシー
Lillian リリアン
Lily リリー
Linda リンダ
Lindsey リンジー
Lisa リサ
Lizette リゼット
Logan ローガン
Lydia リディア
Mackenzie マッケンジー
Macy メイシー
Madeline マデライン
Madison マディソン
Maggie マギー
Makayla マケイラ
Mallory マロリー
Margaret マーガレット
Maria マリア
Mariah マライア
Mariana マリアナ
Marissa マリッサ
Mary メリー、メアリー
Maya マイヤ
Mckenna マッケナ
Megan メーガン
Melanie メラニー
Melissa メリッサ
Mercedes メルセデス
Meredith メレディス
Mia ミア
Michelle ミシェル
Miranda ミランダ

Miriam ミリアム
Molly モリー
Monica モニカ
Monique モニーク
Morgan モーガン
Nadia ナディア
Nancy ナンシー
Naomi ナオミ
Natalia ナタリア
Natalie ナタリー
Natasha ナターシャ
Nia ニア
Nicole ニコール
Nina ニーナ
Olivia オリビア
Paige ペイジ
Paola パオラ
Patricia パトリシア
Peyton ペイトン
Priscilla プリシラ
Rachel レーチェル
Raquel ラケル
Raven レイヴン
Reagan レーガン
Rebecca レベッカ
Renee レネー
Reyna レイナ
Riley ライリー
Robyn ロビン
Rosa ローザ
Rose ローズ
Ruby ルビー
Sabrina サブリナ
Sadie セイディ
Samantha サマンサ
Sandra サンドラ
Sarah サラ、セーラ
Savannah サバンナ
Selena セレーナ
Serena セリーナ
Shania シャニア
Shannon シャノン
Shauna ショウナ
Shayla シェイラ
Shelby シェルビー
Sierra シエラ
Skylar スカイラー
Sophia ソフィア
Sophie ソフィー

Stacy ステイシー
Stephanie ステファニー
Summer サマー
Sydney シドニー
Tabitha タバサ
Talia タリア
Tamara タマラ
Tanya ターニャ
Tara タラ
Tatiana タチアナ

Tara タラ
Taya タヤ
Taylor テイラー
Teresa テレサ
Tessa テッサ
Tiana ティアナ
Tiara ティアラ
Tiffany ティファニー
Tori トーリ
Tyra タイラ

Valeria ヴァレリア
Valerie ヴァレリー
Vanessa ヴァネッサ
Veronica ヴェロニカ
Victoria ビクトリア
Whitney ホイットニー
Yasmine ヤスミン
Yesenia ヤセニア
Zoe ゾーイ

300 Most Common Boys' Names (1998)

Aaron アーロン
Abraham エイブラハム
Adam アダム
Adrian エイドリアン
Aidan エイダン
Alan アラン
Albert アルバート
Alberto アルバートー
Alec アレック
Alejandro アレハンドロ
Alex アレックス
Alexander アレクサンダー
Alexis アレクシス
Alfredo アルフレード
Andre アンドレ
Andres アンドレス
Andrew アンドリュー
Andy アンディ
Angel エンジェル
Angelo アンジェロ
Anthony アンソニー
Antonio アントニオ
Armando アルマンド
Arthur アーサー
Arturo アルツーロ
Ashton アシュトン
Austin オースティン
Avery エィヴェリー
Bailey ベイリー
Benjamin ベンジャミン
Blake ブレーク
Braden ブレーデン
Bradley ブラッドリー
Brady ブレイディ
Brandon ブランドン
Brendan ブレンダン

Brennan ブレナン
Brent ブレント
Brett ブレット
Brian ブライアン
Brock ブロック
Bryant ブライアント
Bryce ブライス
Bryson ブライソン
Cade ケイド
Caleb ケイレブ
Calvin カルビン
Cameron キャメロン
Carl カール
Carlos カーロス
Carson カーソン
Carter カーター
Casey ケイシー
Cesar シーザー
Chad チャッド
Chance チャンス
Chandler チャンドラー
Charles チャールズ
Chase チェイス
Christian クリスチャン
Christopher クリストファー
Clayton クレイトン
Cody コーディー
Colby コルビー
Cole コール
Colin コリン
Colton コルトン
Connor コナー
Cooper クーパー
Corbin コービン
Corey コーリー
Craig クレーグ

Curtis カーティス
Dakota ダコタ
Dallas ダラス
Dalton ダルトン
Damian デイミアン
Damon デイモン
Daniel ダニエル
Danny ダニー
Dante ダンテ
Darian ダリアン
Darius ダリアス
Darrell ダレル
Darren ダーレン
David デビッド、デイヴィッド
Dawson ダーソン
Deandre デアンドレ
Dennis デニス
Deonte デアンテ
Derek デレク
Deshawn デショーン
Devin デビン
Devonte デヴォンテ
Diego ディエゴ
Dominic ドミニク
Donald ドナルド
Donovan ドノヴァン
Douglas ダグラス
Drake ドレーク
Drew ドルー
Dustin ダスティン
Dylan ディラン
Eddie エディ
Edgar エドガー
Eduardo エドワルド
Edward エドワード
Edwin エドウィン

Eli イーライ
Elias イライアス
Elijah イライジャ
Elliot エリオット
Emmanuel イマニュエル
Enrique エンリケ
Eric エリック
Esteban エステバン
Ethan イーサン
Evan エバン
Fabian ファビアン
Fernando フェルナンド
Francisco フランシスコ
Frank フランク
Frederick フレドリック
Gabriel ガブリエル
Gage ゲイジ
Garrett ガレット
Gary ゲーリー
Gavin ギャビン
George ジョージ
Gerardo ジェラルド
Giovanni ジョバンニ
Grant グラント
Grayson グレイソン
Gregory グレゴリー
Griffin グリフィン
Harrison ハリソン
Hayden ヘイデン
Hector ヘクター
Henry ヘンリー
Hunter ハンター
Ian イアン
Isaac アイザック
Isaiah アイザーヤ
Ismael イシマイル
Israel イスラエル
Ivan アイヴァン
Jack ジャック
Jackson ジャクソン
Jacob ジェイコブ
Jaden ジェイデン
Jaime ジェイミー
Jake ジェイク
Jalen ジェイレン
James ジェイムス
Jared ジェレッド
Jarrett ジェレット

Jason ジェイソン
Javon ジャヴォン
Jay ジェイ
Jeffrey ジェフリー
Jeremiah ジェレマイヤ
Jeremy ジェレミー
Jerry ジェリー
Jesse ジェシー
Jesus ヘスース
Jimmy ジミー
Joe ジョー
Joel ジョエル
John ジョン
Johnny ジョニー
Jonah ジョナ
Jonathan ジョナサン
Jordan ジョルダン
Jorge ホルヘ
Jose ホゼ
Joseph ジョセフ
Joshua ジョシュア
Josiah ジョサイア
Josue ジョズエ
Juan ワン
Julian ジュリアン
Julio フリオ
Justice ジャスティス
Justin ジャスティン
Kaden ケイデン
Keegan キーガン
Keith キース
Kenneth ケネス
Kevin ケビン
Kobe コービー
Kylar カイラー
Kyle カイル
Landon ランドン
Lane レーン
Larry ラリー
Lawrence ローレンス
Leonardo レオナルド
Levi リーバイ
Liam リアム
Logan ローガン
Lorenzo ロレンソ
Louis ルイス
Lucas ルーカス
Luis ルイス

Luke ルーク
Malik マリク
Manuel マヌエル
Marco マルコ
Marcos マルコス
Marcus マーカス
Mario マリオ
Mark マーク
Martin マーティン
Mason メイソン
Matthew マシュー
Max マックス
Maxwell マクスウェル
Micah マイカ
Michael マイケル
Miguel ミゲール
Miles マイルズ
Mitchell ミッチェル
Mohammad モハメッド
Morgan モーガン
Nathan ネーサン
Nathaniel ナサニエル
Nicholas ニコラス
Noah ノア
Nolan ノーラン
Omar オマー
Oscar オスカー
Owen オーエン
Pablo パブロ
Parker パーカー
Patrick パトリック
Paul ポール
Pedro ペドロ
Peter ピーター
Peyton ペイトン
Phillip フィリップ
Preston プレストン
Quentin クエンティン
Quinton クイントン
Rafael ラファエル
Ramon ラモン
Randy ランディ
Raul ラウル
Raymond レイモンド
Reece リース
Reid リード
Ricardo リカルド
Richard リチャード

Ricky リッキー
Riley ライリー
Robert ロバート
Roberto ロベルト
Ronald ロナルド
Ruben ルベン
Russell ラッセル
Ryan ライアン
Samuel サミュエル
Scott スコット
Sean ショーン
Sebastian セバスチャン
Sergio セルジオ
Seth セス
Shane シェーン
Skyler スカイラー
Spencer スペンサー
Steven スティーヴン
Tanner タナー
Taylor テイラー
Terrance テランス
Terrell テレル
Theodore セオドア
Thomas トマス
Timothy ティモシー
Tommy トミー
Tony トニー
Travis トラビス
Trent トレント
Trenton トレントン
Trevon トラヴォン
Trevor トレヴァー
Trey トレイ
Tristan トリスタン
Troy トロイ
Tucker タカー
Ty タイ
Tyler タイラー
Tyrek タイリク
Victor ヴィクター
Vincent ヴィンセント
Wesley ウェスリー
William ウィリアム
Wyatt ワイアット
Xavier ザビエル
Zachariah ザカライヤ
Zachary ザカリー
Zane ゼイン

SECTION ONE

The Basic 46 Katakana Characters

ア a	イ i	ウ u	エ e	オ o
カ ka	キ ki	ク ku	ケ ke	コ ko
サ sa	シ shi	ス su	セ se	ソ so
タ ta	チ chi	ツ tsu	テ te	ト to
ナ na	ニ ni	ヌ nu	ネ ne	ノ no
ハ ha (wa)*	ヒ hi	フ fu	ヘ he (e)*	ホ ho
マ ma	ミ mi	ム mu	メ me	モ mo
ヤ ya		ユ yu		ヨ yo
ラ ra	リ ri	ル ru	レ re	ロ ro
ワ wa				ヲ o**
ン n				

* These characters are pronounced differently when they are used as grammatical particles.

** This character is only used as a grammatical particle. It is not used to write words.

"**a**" as in f**a**ther

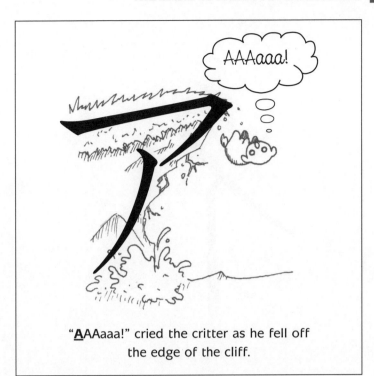

"**A**AAaaa!" cried the critter as he fell off the edge of the cliff.

Writing Tip "a" has two strokes and both are brushes.

Trace these characters.

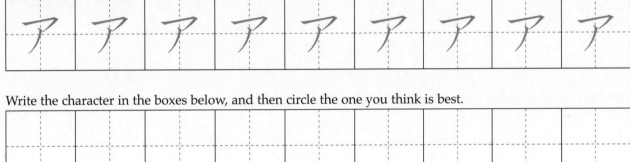

Write the character in the boxes below, and then circle the one you think is best.

1. **a me ri ka** (America; United States)

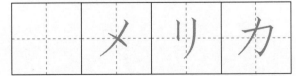

2. **su ko a** (score)

3. **e a ko n** (air conditioner; air conditioning)

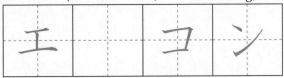

4. **ā to** (art)

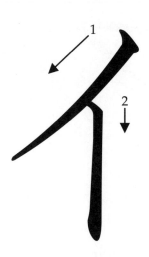

"**i**" as in **ea**sy

An **ea**sel holds your picture while you work on it or display it.

Writing Tip "**i**" has two strokes: 1) a brush and 2) stop.

Trace these characters.

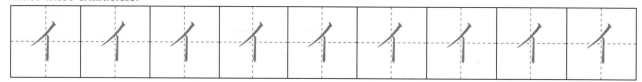

Write the character in the boxes below, and then circle the one you think is best.

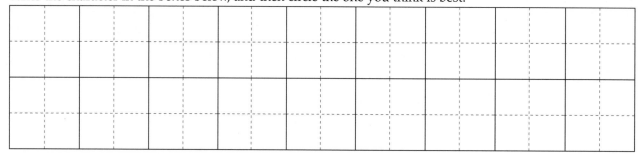

1. **to i re** (toilet)

2. **a i ro n** (iron)

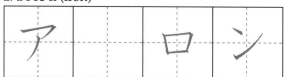

3. **na i fu** (knife)

4. **i gi ri su** (England)

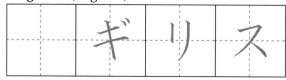

"**Oo**oo!" The water balloon was cold as it splashed on his back!

"**u**" as in y**ou**

Writing Tip "**u**" has three strokes: 1) a stop, 2) stop and 3) brush.

Trace these characters.

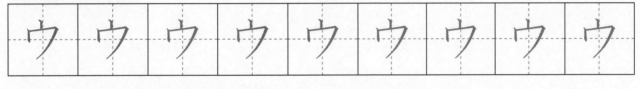

Write the character in the boxes below, and then circle the one you think is best.

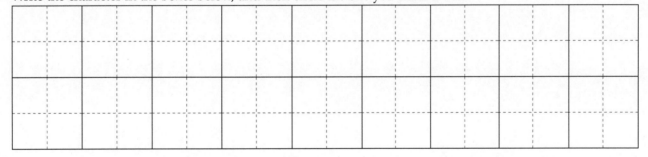

1. **u i ru su** ((computer) virus)

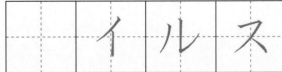

2. **ki u i** (kiwi)

3. **ma u su** ((computer) mouse)

4. **ū ru** (wool)

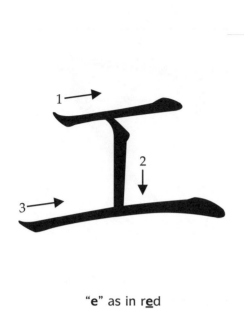

"**e**" as in r<u>e</u>d

<u>e</u>levator doors

Writing Tip "**e**" has three strokes and they are all stops.

Trace these characters.

Write the character in the boxes below, and then circle the one you think is best.

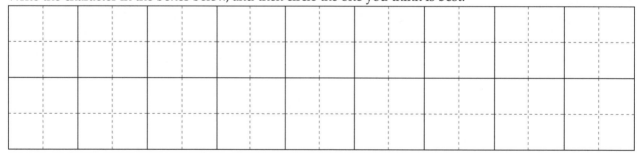

1. **u ē tā** (waiter)

2. **e rā** ((computer) error)

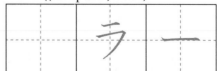

3. **e su sa i zu** (small; "S" size)

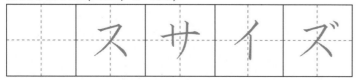

4. **e i zu** (AIDS)

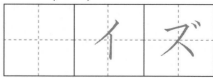

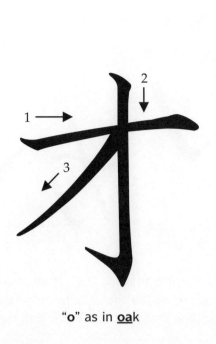

"o" as in <u>oa</u>k

an <u>O</u>lympic figure skater

Writing Tip "o" has three strokes: 1) a stop, 2) jump and 3) brush.

Trace these characters.

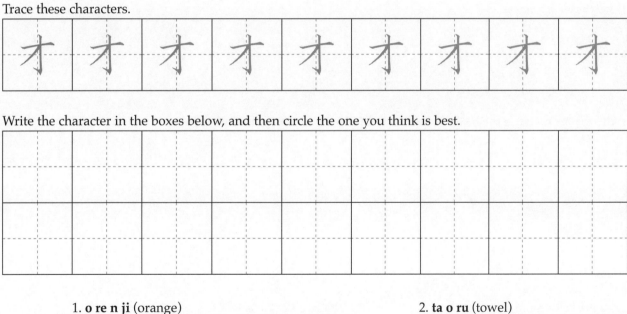

Write the character in the boxes below, and then circle the one you think is best.

1. **o re n ji** (orange)

	レ	ン	ジ

2. **ta o ru** (towel)

	タ		ル

3. **o ru gan** (organ – musical instrument)

	ル	ガ	ン

4. **o i ru** (oil)

		イ	ル

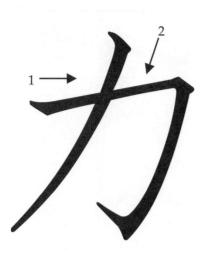

Katakana "**ka**" カ and hiragana "**ka**" か look alike, except that katakana "**ka**" has one fewer stroke, and its lines are straighter and more angular.

"**ka**" as in **ca**r

Writing Tip "ka" has two strokes: 1) a jump and 2) brush.

Trace these characters.

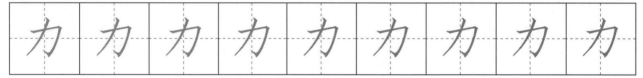

Write the character in the boxes below, and then circle the one you think is best.

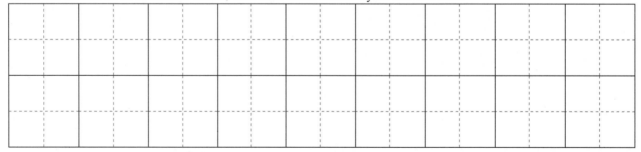

1. **ka me ra** (camera)

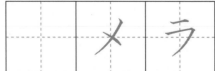

2. **ka ra o ke** (karaoke)

3. **ka ta ka na** (katakana characters)

4. **ka na da** (Canada)

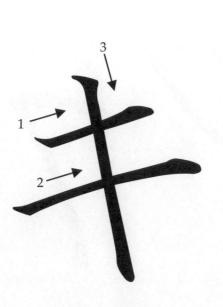

"ki" as in <u>key</u>

Katakana "**ki**" キ and hiragana "*ki*" き look alike, except that katakana "**ki**" has one fewer stroke, and it does not have a "jump" stroke.

Writing Tip "ki" has three strokes and they are all stops.

Trace these characters.

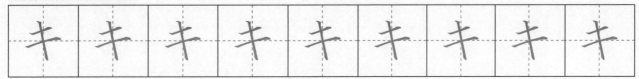

Write the character in the boxes below, and then circle the one you think is best.

1. **su tē ki** (steak)

2. **me ki shi ko** (Mexico)

3. **ho chi ki su** (stapler – Hotchkiss)

4. **su ki i** (ski; skiing)

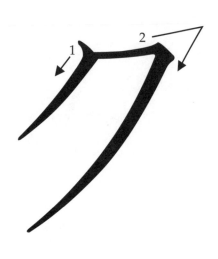

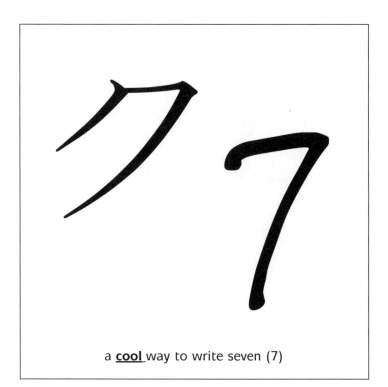

"ku" as in cuc<u>koo</u>

a <u>**cool**</u> way to write seven (7)

Writing Tip "ku" has two strokes and both are brushes.

Trace these characters.

Write the character in the boxes below, and then circle the one you think is best.

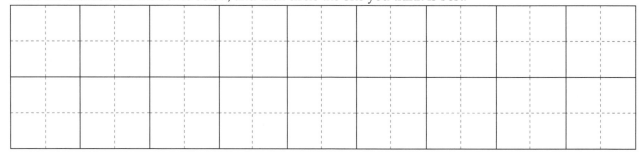

1. **pi n ku** (pink)

2. **ku ra su** (class)

3. **ta ku shi i** (taxi)

4. **ba i ku** (motorcycle)

"ke" as in **Ke**vin

a **ka**ngaroo

Writing Tip : "**ke**" has three strokes: 1) a brush, 2) stop and 3) brush.

Trace these characters.

Write the character in the boxes below, and then circle the one you think is best.

1. **su ke bō** (skateboard; to skateboard)

2. **kē ki** (cake)

3. **su kē to** (skates; to skate)

4. **ke ni a** (Kenya)

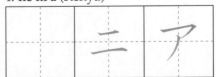

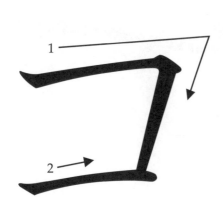

"**ko**" as in <u>co</u>coa

a cup of hot <u>co</u>coa

Writing Tip "ko" has two strokes and both are stops.

Trace these characters.

Write the character in the boxes below, and then circle the one you think is best.

1. **ko n sā to** (concert)

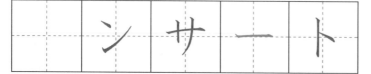

2. **kō chi** (coach)

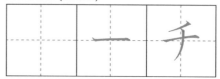

3. **kō hii** (coffee)

4. **kō to** (coat; (tennis) court)

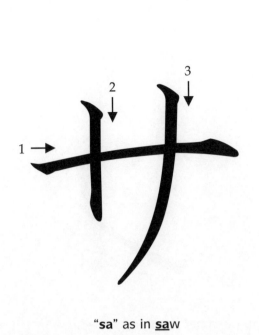

"**sa**" as in **sa**w

A **saw**horse holds wood while you cut it.

Writing Tip "**sa**" has three strokes: 1) a stop, 2) stop and 3) brush.

Trace these characters.

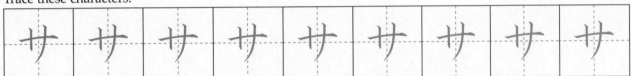

Write the character in the boxes below, and then circle the one you think is best.

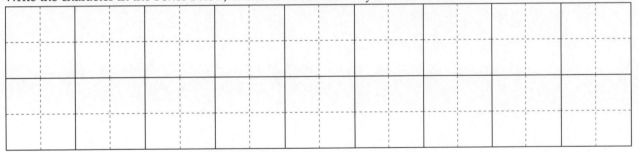

1. **sa i n** (signature; autograph)

2. **sā ka su** (circus)

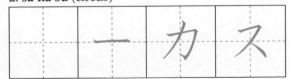

3. **sā chi** (search)

4. **sa n da ru** (sandals)

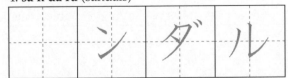

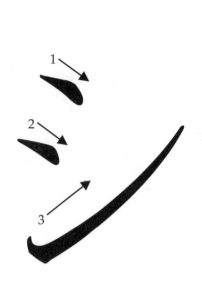

"**shi**" as in <u>she</u>

<u>She</u> tilted her head and smiled.

Writing Tip "shi" has three strokes: 1) a stop, 2) stop and 3) brush.

Trace these characters.

Write the character in the boxes below, and then circle the one you think is best.

1. **shi ri a** (Syria)

2. **mi shi n** (sewing machine)

3. **shi ru bā shi i to**
   (Silver Seat – reserved seating on public transportation for the elderly, handicapped, and so on.)

"su" as in **su**per

It's **Su**perman, er super-critter.

Writing Tip "**su**" has two strokes: 1) a brush and 2) stop.

Trace these characters.

Write the character in the boxes below, and then circle the one you think is best.

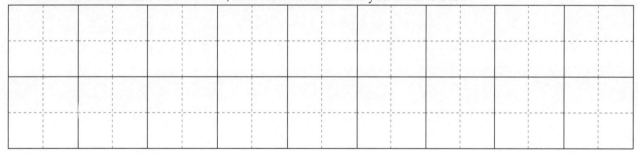

1. **su kā to** (skirt)

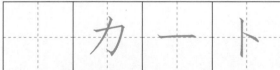

2. **su te re o** (stereo)

3. **ku ri su ma su** (Christmas)

4. **ki su** (kiss)

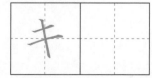

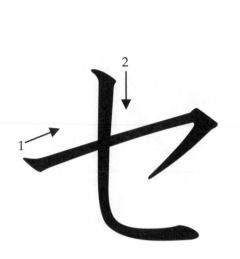

"**se**" as in **se**t

Katakana "**se**" and hiragana "**se**" look a little alike.

Writing Tip "**se**" has two strokes: 1) a brush and 2) stop.

Trace these characters.

Write the character in the boxes below, and then circle the one you think is best.

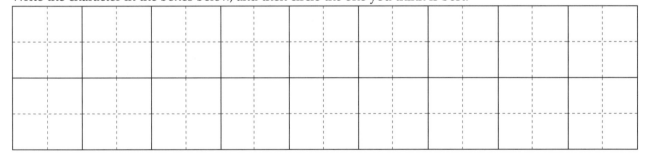

1. **sē tā** (sweater)

2. **sē ru** (sale)

3. **se ro ri** (celery)

4. **se i kō** (Seiko watch corporation)

A kid (goat) got into a fight after school, and he got an eye knocked out! The next day when other kid (goats) pointed and said, "You've only got one eye," he said, "**So**!"

"**so**" as in <u>so</u>

Writing Tip "**so**" has two strokes: 1) a stop and 2) brush.

Trace these characters.

Write the character in the boxes below, and then circle the one you think is best.

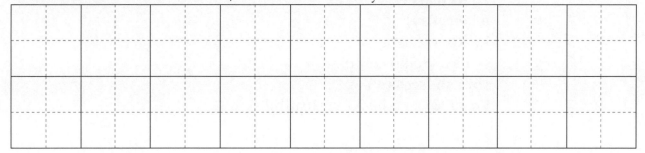

1. **shi i sō** (seesaw)

2. **so fa** (sofa)

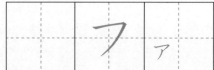

3. **so u ru** (Seoul, Korea; soul)

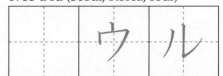

4. **sō da** (soda)

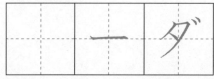

READING PRACTICE 1: ア ～ ソ

You should be able to read the words below now. Fold the page lengthwise (or cover it with your hand) so you can only see the katakana words on the left hand side. Try reading them aloud and then check with the words on the right. Keep practicing until you can read them all. For an extra challenge try reading the Japanese and saying the English word before checking.

Note: In katakana long vowels are written with a line (ー) called **bō**, rather than writing one of the five vowels as in hiragana. In this way, katakana writing is simpler than hiragana writing. Several of the example words below have long vowels. In order to improve your pronunciation, be sure to pronounce the long vowels with approximately twice the length of a single syllable.

ア イ ス	**a i su** (ice)
ス コ ア	**su ko a** (score)
ア ク セ ス	**a ku se su** (access)
イ カ	**i ka** (squid)
サ イ	**sa i** (rhino)
キ ウ イ	**ki u i** (kiwi)
エ キ ス	**e ki su** (extract)
オ ス カ ー	**o su kā** (the Oscar)
オ ア シ ス	**o a shi su** (oasis)
サ ー カ ス	**sā ka su** (circus)
キ ス	**ki su** (kiss)
ス イ ス	**su i su** (Switzerland)
カ ー キ	**kā ki** (khaki color)
ス キ ー	**su ki i** (to ski; skiing)
サ ク セ ス	**sa ku se su** (success)
ケ ー キ	**kē ki** (cake)
オ ー ケ ー	**ō kē** (okay)
コ コ ア	**ko ko a** (cocoa)
セ イ コ ー	**se i kō** (Seiko company)
シ ー ソ ー	**shi i sō** (seesaw)
コ ソ コ ソ	**ko so ko so** (sneakily; stealthily)

Romaji pronunciation guide:
a   as in father and bother
i   as in Hawaii and beat
u   as in glue and youth
e   as in red and bed
o   as in oak and bone

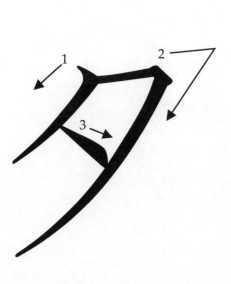

"ta" as in t**a**ll

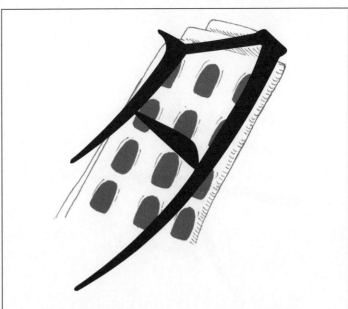

the leaning **to**wer of Pisa (In Japanese "tower" is pronounced with a "**ta**" as in t**a**ll).

Writing Tip "**ta**" has tree strokes: 1) a brush, 2) brush and 3) stop.

Trace these characters.

Write the character in the boxes below, and then circle the one you think is best.

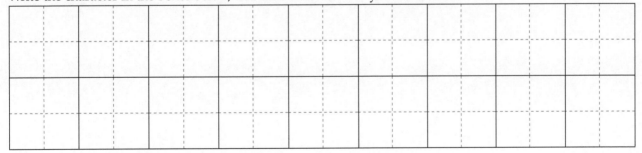

1. **ta i** (Thailand; tie)

2. **sē tā** (sweater)

3. **ta ku shi i** (taxi)

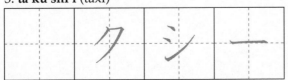

4. **ta ko su** (taco)

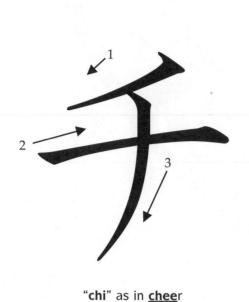

"**chi**" as in **chee**r

a **chee**rleader

Writing Tip "**chi**" has three strokes: 1) a brush, 2) stop and 3) brush.

Trace these characters.

Write the character in the boxes below, and then circle the one you think is best.

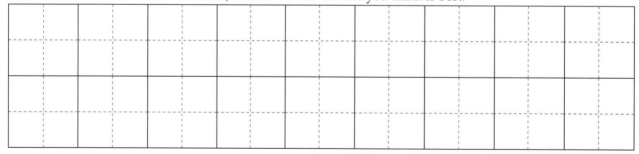

1. **chi ki n** ((cooked) chicken)

2. **se n chi** (centimeter)

3. **i n chi** (inch)

4. **kō chi** (coach)

"tsu" as in ca**ts**

Two children are sliding down a slide.
("**ts**" like ca**ts** and "**u**" like y**ou**)

Writing Tip "tsu" has three strokes: 1) a stop 2) stop and 3) brush. (Note: **tsu** ツ and **shi** シ look alike, but the strokes in **tsu** go downward, and the strokes in **shi** go more to the right)

Trace these characters.

Write the character in the boxes below, and then circle the one you think is best.

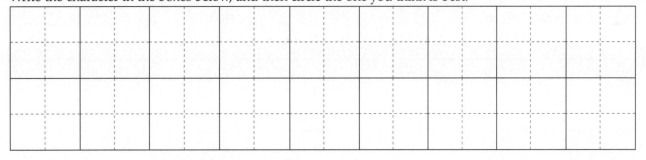

1. sū tsu (suit)

2. tsu ā (tour)

3. shi i tsu ((bed)sheet)

4. ta i tsu (tights)

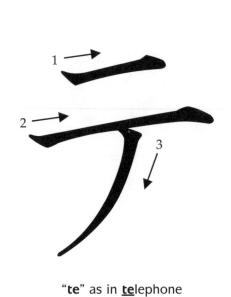

"**te**" as in **te**lephone

a **te**lephone pole and wires

Writing Tip "te" has three strokes: 1) a stop, 2) stop and 3) brush

Trace these characters.

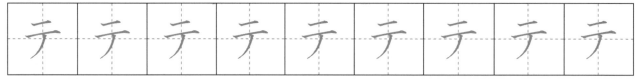

Write the character in the boxes below, and then circle the one you think is best.

1. **kā te n** (curtains)

2. **te ki su to** (textbook)

3. **te ku** (tech — abbr.)

4. **ā ki te ku to** (architect)

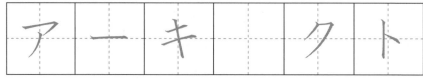

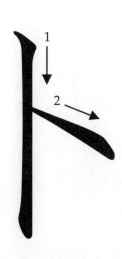

"**to**" as in **to**tem

a **to**tem pole

Writing Tip "**to**" has two strokes and they are both stops.

Trace these characters.

Write the character in the boxes below, and then circle the one you think is best.

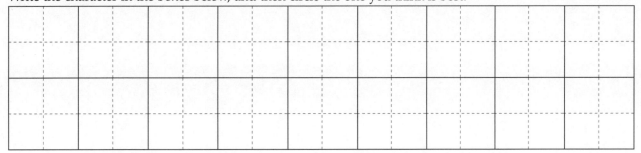

1. **su kā to** (skirt)

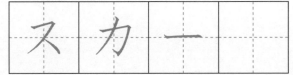

2. **te su to** (test)

3. **sa i to** ((web or real) site)

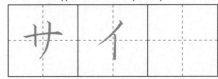

4. **su tā to** (start)

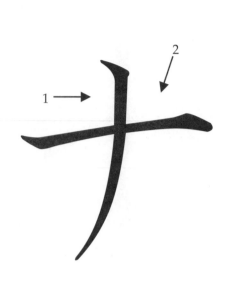

"**na**" as in **no**t

a knife

Writing Tip "**na**" has two strokes: 1) a stop and 2) brush.

Trace these characters.

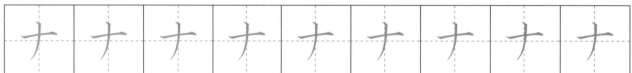

Write the character in the boxes below, and then circle the one you think is best.

1. **na i fu** (knife)

2. **na rē tā** (narrator)

3. **tsu na** (tuna)

4. **sa u na** (sauna)

5. **na sa** (NASA)

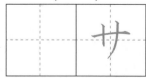

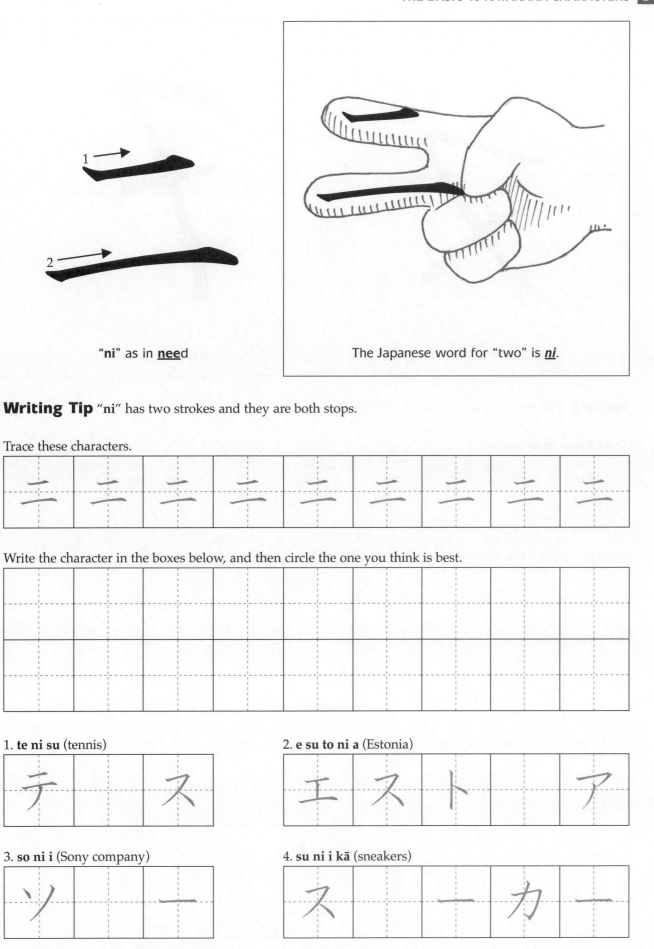

"ni" as in **nee**d

The Japanese word for "two" is *ni*.

Writing Tip "ni" has two strokes and they are both stops.

Trace these characters.

Write the character in the boxes below, and then circle the one you think is best.

1. te ni su (tennis)

2. e su to ni a (Estonia)

3. so ni i (Sony company)

4. su ni i kā (sneakers)

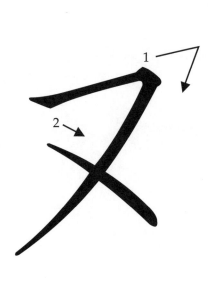

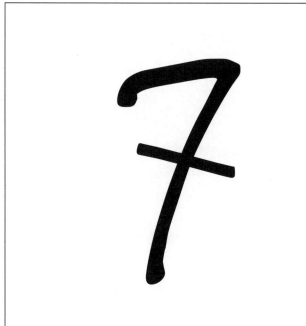

"**nu**" as in **new**

a **new** way to write seven (7)

Writing Tip "**nu**" has two strokes: 1) a brush and 2) stop.

Trace these characters.

Write the character in the boxes below and then circle the one you think is best.

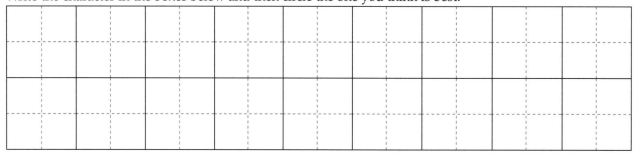

1. **a i nu** (Ainu – indigenous people of Japan)

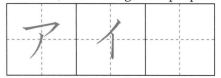

2. **su nū pi i** (Snoopy)

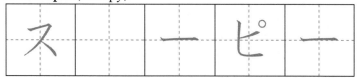

3. **nū do ru** (noodles)

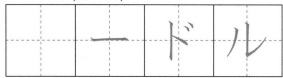

4. **ka nū** (canoe)

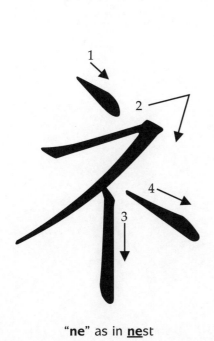

"ne" as in **ne**st

a **ne**st on top of a tree

Writing Tip "ne" has four strokes: 1) a stop, 2) brush, 3) stop and 4) stop.

Trace these characters.

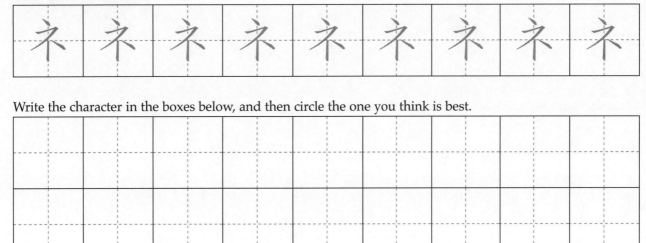

Write the character in the boxes below, and then circle the one you think is best.

1. **i n tā ne tto** (internet)

2. **ne ga** ((photo) negatives)

3. **to n ne ru** (tunnel)

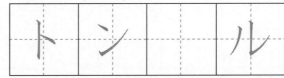

"**no**" as in **no**se

a **no**se

Writing Tip "**no**" has only one stroke and it is a brush.

Trace these characters.

Write the character in the boxes below, and then circle the one you think is best.

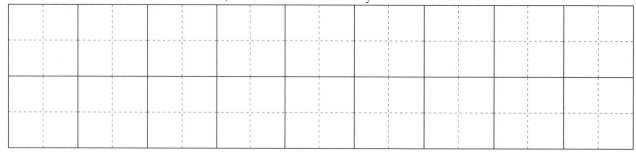

1. **nō to** (notebook)

2. **pi a no** (piano)

3. **ka ji no** (casino)

4. **su nō bō do** (snowboard; snowboarding)

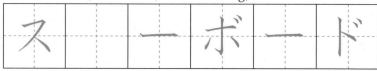

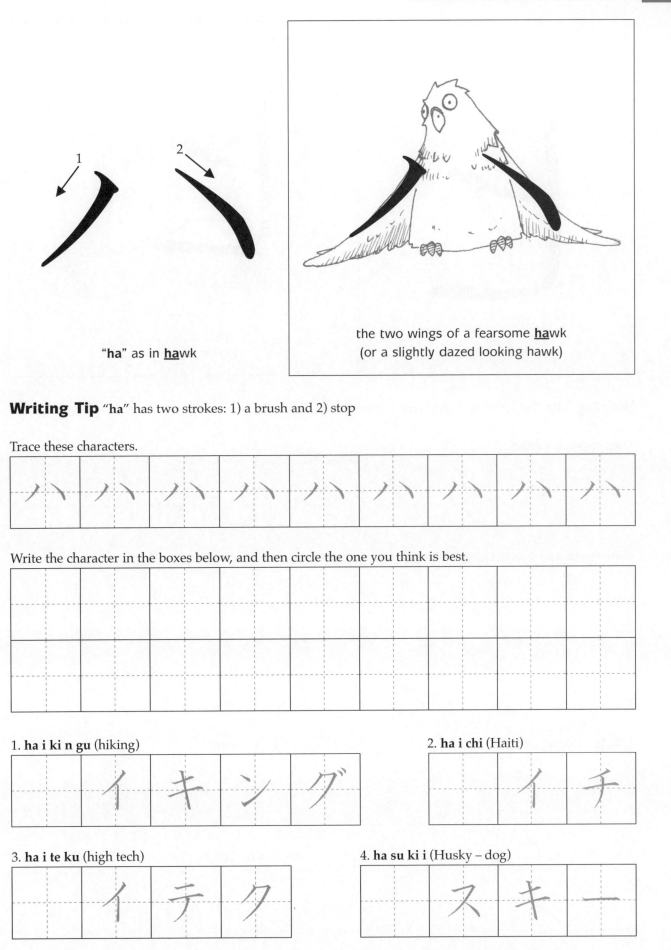

"ha" as in <u>ha</u>wk

the two wings of a fearsome <u>ha</u>wk
(or a slightly dazed looking hawk)

Writing Tip "**ha**" has two strokes: 1) a brush and 2) stop

Trace these characters.

Write the character in the boxes below, and then circle the one you think is best.

1. ha i ki n gu (hiking)

イ キ ン グ

2. ha i chi (Haiti)

イ チ

3. ha i te ku (high tech)

イ テ ク

4. ha su ki i (Husky – dog)

ス キ ー

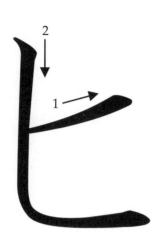

"**hi**" as in <u>he</u>

<u>He</u> drives the car.

Writing Tip "**hi**" has two strokes and they are both stops.

Trace these characters.

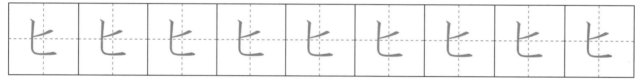

Write the character in the boxes below, and then circle the one you think is best.

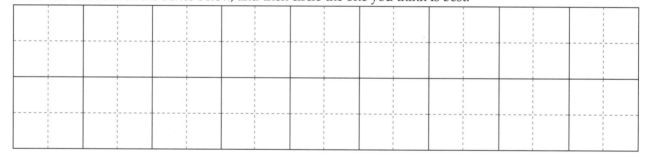

1. **kō hi i** (coffee)

2. **hi n to** (hint)

3. **hi i tā** (heater)

4. **hi i rō** (hero)

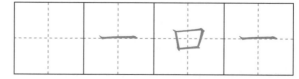

"**fu**" as in <u>Hoot!</u>
(except the lips are less rounded,
and more air escapes from the mouth)

The owl cries, "<u>Hoot</u>! <u>Hoot</u>!"

Writing Tip "**fu**" has only one stroke and it is a brush.

Trace these characters.

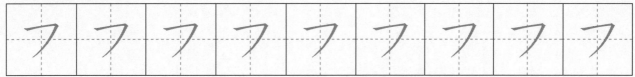

Write the character in the boxes below, and then circle the one you think is best.

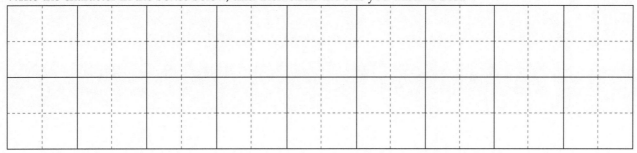

1. **su kā fu** (scarf)

2. **fu ra n su** (France)

3. **so fu to** (software)

4. **go ru fu** (golf)

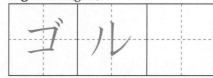

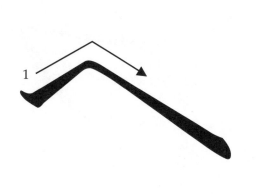

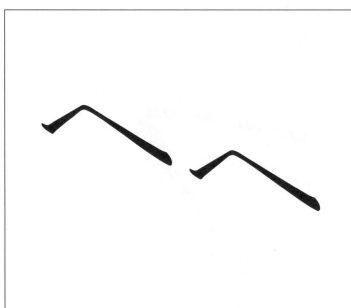

"**he**" as in **he**lp

There are no significant differences between katakana "**he**" and hiragana "**he**."

Writing Tip "**he**" has only one stroke and it is a stop.

Trace these characters.

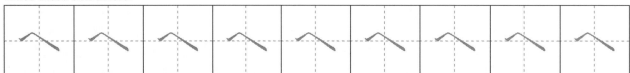

Write the character in the boxes below, and then circle the one you think is best.

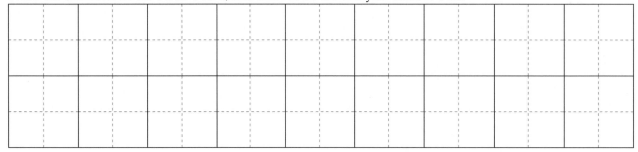

1. **he** ri (helicopter)

2. **he** ddo hō n (headphones)

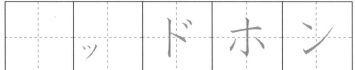

3. **he** ru pu (help)

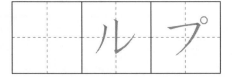

4. **he** a ka rā (hair dye; hair coloring)

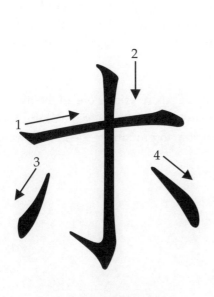

"ho" as in <u>Ho</u>! <u>Ho</u>!

Mr. "<u>Ho Ho</u>" laughs even when stuck in a chimney!

Writing Tip "ho" has four strokes: 1) a stop, 2) jump, 3) stop and 4) stop.

Trace these characters.

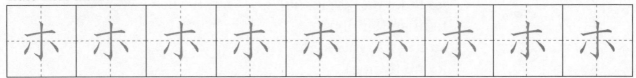

Write the character in the boxes below, and then circle the one you think is best.

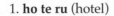

1. **ho te ru** (hotel)

2. **ho kkē** (hockey)

3. **hō mu** ((train station) platform)

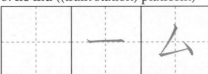

4. **ho i ru** (foil)

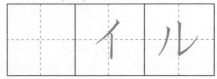

READING PRACTICE 2: タ 〜 ホ

You should be able to read the words below now. Fold the page lengthwise (or cover it with your hand) so you can only see the katakana words on the left hand side. Try reading them aloud and then check with the words on the right. Keep practicing until you can read them all. For an extra challenge try reading the Japanese and saying the English word before checking.

Note: In katakana long vowels are written with a line (ー) called **bō**, rather than writing one of the five vowels as in hiragana. In this way, katakana writing is simpler than hiragana writing. Several of the example words below have long vowels. In order to improve your pronunciation, be sure to pronounce the long vowels with approximately twice the length of a single syllable.

左						右
タ ク シ ー						**ta ku shi i** (taxi)
タ コ ス						**ta ko su** (taco)
コ ー チ						**kō chi** (coach)
ス ー ツ						**sū tsu** (suit)
ツ ア ー						**tsu ā** (tour)
テ キ ス ト						**te ki su to** (textbook)
ス カ ー ト						**su kā to** (skirt)
テ ス ト						**te su to** (test)
ナ イ フ						**na i fu** (knife)
ツ ナ						**tsu na** (tuna)
カ タ カ ナ						**ka ta ka na** (katakana)
テ ニ ス						**te ni su** (tennis)
ス ニ ー カ ー						**su ni i kā** (sneakers)
カ ヌ ー						**ka nū** (canoe)
ア イ ヌ						**a i nu** (Ainu – Indigenous people of northern Japan)
ノ ー ト						**nō to** (notebook)
ハ ス キ ー						**ha su ki i** (husky – dog)
コ ー ヒ ー						**kō hi i** (coffee)
ヒ ン ト						**hi n to** (hint)
ソ フ ト						**so fu to** (software)
ヘ リ						**he ri** (helicopter)
ホ テ ル						**ho te ru** (hotel)

Romaji pronunciation guide:	
a	as in father and bother
i	as in Hawaii and beat
u	as in glue and youth
e	as in red and bed
o	as in oak and bone

"**ma**" as in **mo**m

Mom holds Baby while
she attends to some work.

Writing Tip "**ma**" has two strokes: 1) a brush and 2) stop.

Trace these characters.

Write the character in the boxes below, and then circle the one you think is best.

1. **to ma to** (tomato)

2. **mā kā** (marker)

3. **ma i ku** (microphone)

4. **ma i ru** (mile)

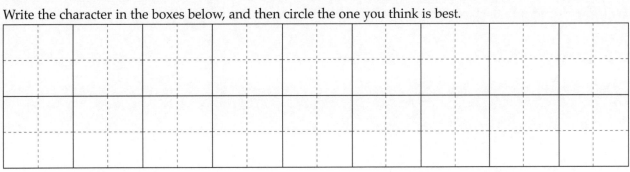

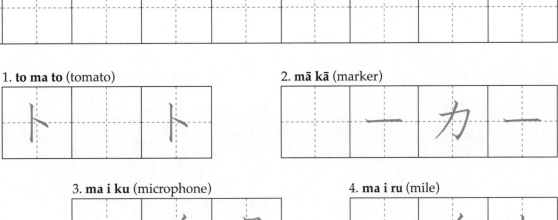

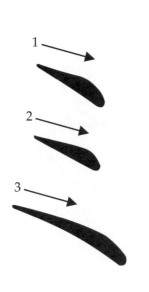

"**mi**" as in **me**ow

A cat's three whiskers, "**Me**ow!"

Writing Tip "**mi**" has three strokes and all three are stops.

Trace these characters.

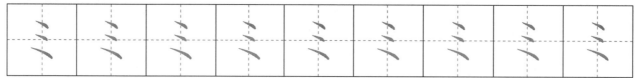

Write the character in the boxes below, and then circle the one you think is best.

1. **mi ki sā** (blender)

2. **sa ra mi** (salami)

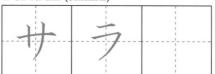

3. **mi ni kā** (toy car)

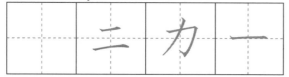

4. **mi i ra** (mummy; from Portuguese)

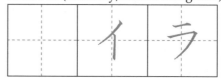

"**mu**" as in **moo**

I love ja**mu** (jam)!

Writing Tip "mu" has two strokes and both are stops.

Trace these characters.

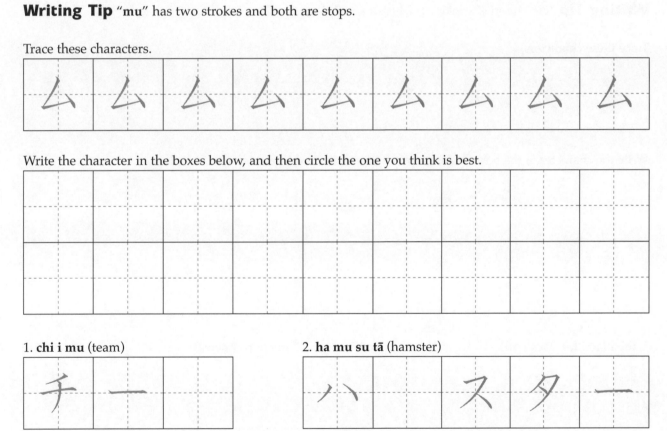

Write the character in the boxes below, and then circle the one you think is best.

1. **chi i mu** (team)

2. **ha mu su tā** (hamster)

3. **hō mu su te i** (home stay)

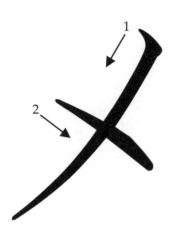

"**me**" as in **Me**xico

the "**X**" in **Me**xico

Writing Tip "**me**" has two strokes: 1) a brush and 2) stop.

Trace these characters.

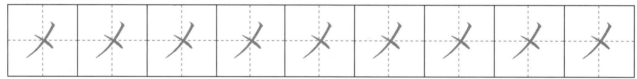

Write the character in the boxes below, and then circle the one you think is best.

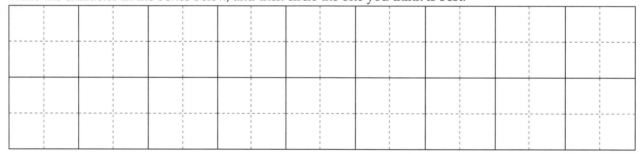

1. **me ki shi ko** (Mexico)

2. **mē to ru** (meter)

3. **a ni me** (Japanese cartoons)

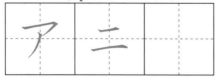

4. **me mo** (memo; notes)

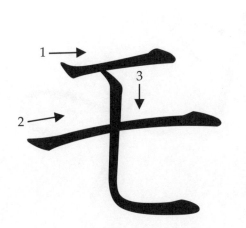

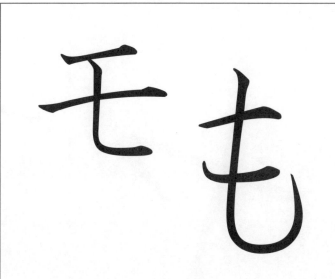

"**mo**" as in **mo**re

Hiragana "*mo*" and katakana "**mo**" look a bit alike.
Note that stroke #3 does not go through stroke #1.

Writing Tip "**mo**" has three strokes and they are all stops.

Trace these characters.

Write the character in the boxes below, and then circle the one you think is best.

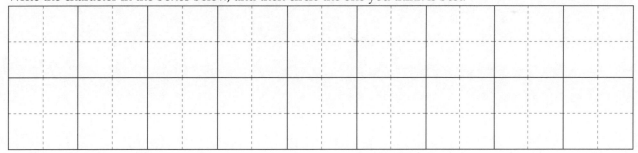

1. **sā mo n** (salmon – fish)

2. **shi na mo n** (cinnamon)

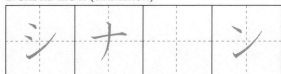

3. **mo ni tā** (monitor)

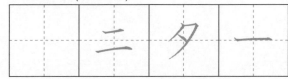

4. **mō ru** (mall)

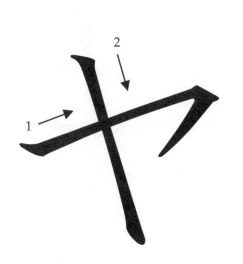

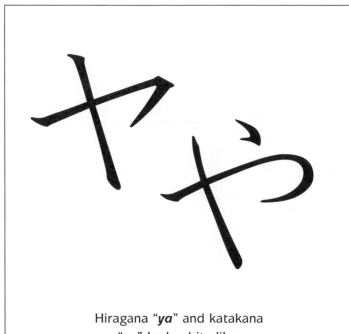

"**ya**" as in <u>ya</u>rn

Hiragana "**ya**" and katakana
"**ya**" look a bit alike.

Writing Tip "ya" has two strokes: 1) a brush and 2) stop.

Trace these characters.

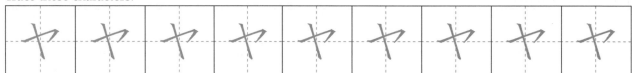

Write the character in the boxes below, and then circle the one you think is best.

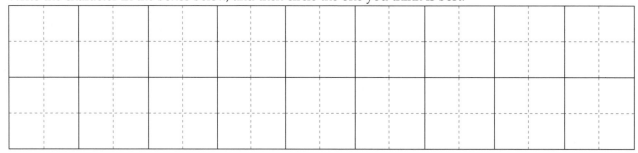

1. **ta i ya** (tire)

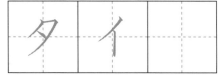

2. **i ya ho n** (earphones)

3. **da i ya** (daimond)

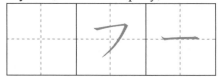

4. **ya fū** (Yahoo – company)

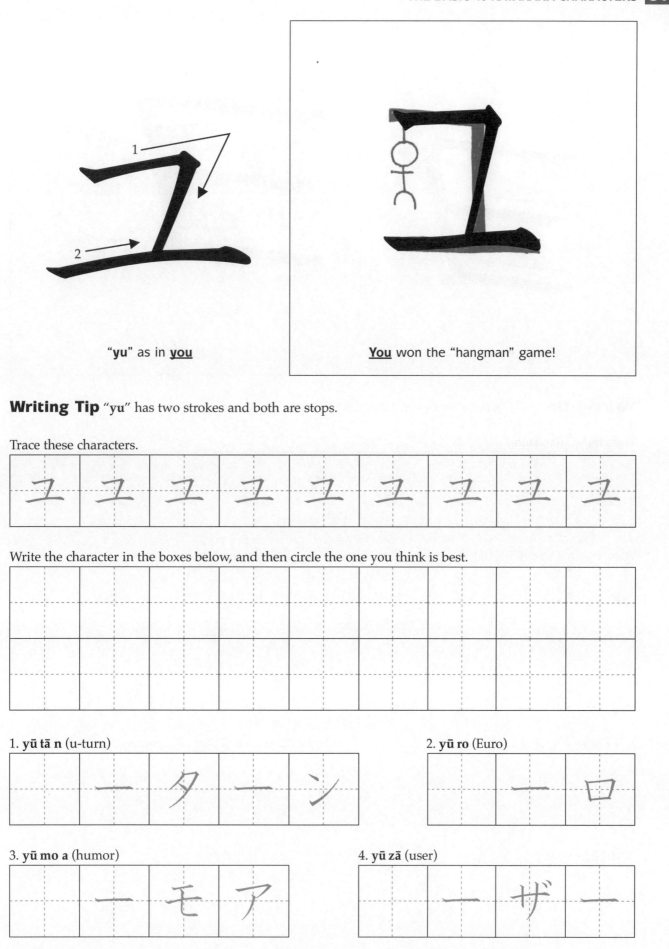

"**yu**" as in **you**

You won the "hangman" game!

Writing Tip "yu" has two strokes and both are stops.

Trace these characters.

Write the character in the boxes below, and then circle the one you think is best.

1. yū tā n (u-turn)

2. yū ro (Euro)

3. yū mo a (humor)

4. yū zā (user)

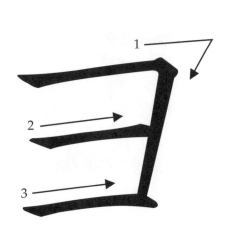

"**yo**" as in **yo**gurt   **yo**gurt

Writing Tip "**yo**" has three strokes and they are all stops.

Trace these characters.

Write the character in the boxes below, and then circle the one you think is best.

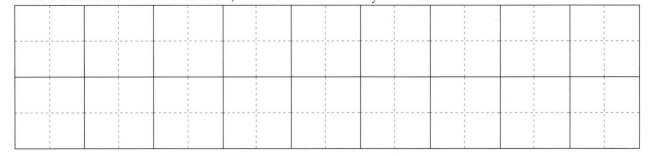

1. **ku re yo n** (crayon)

2. **to yo ta** (Toyota – company)

3. **yō yō** (yo-yo)

4. **yō ga** (yoga)

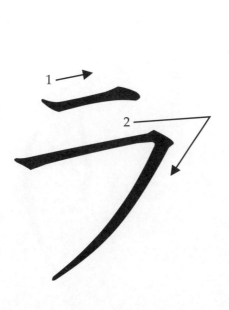

"**ra**" as in **ro**bber

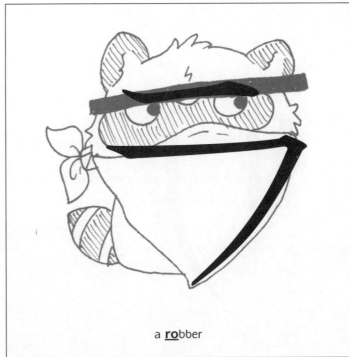

a **ro**bber

Writing Tip "**ra**" has two strokes: 1) a stop and 2) brush.

Trace these characters.

Write the character in the boxes below, and then circle the one you think is best.

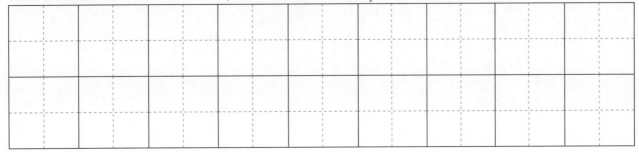

1. **ka me ra** (camera)

2. **ku ra su** (school class)

3. **hō mu ra n** (homerun)

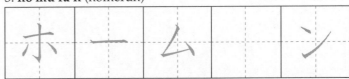

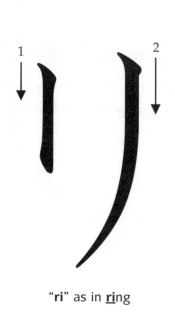

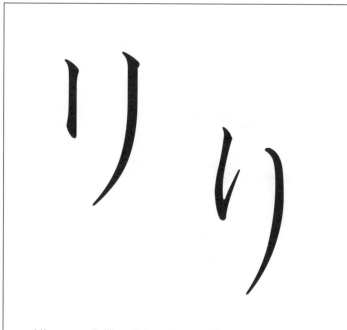

"**ri**" as in **ri**ng

Hiragana "**ri**" and katakana "**ri**" look a bit alike.

Writing Tip "**ri**" has two strokes: 1) a stop and 2) brush.

Trace these characters.

Write the character in the boxes below, and then circle the one you think is best.

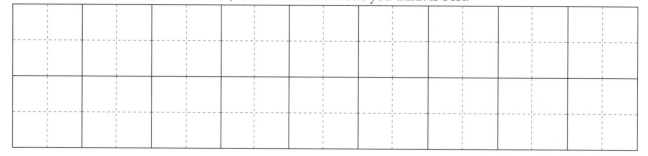

1. **a fu ri ka** (Africa)

2. **i ta ri a** (Italy)

3. **a i su ku ri i mu** (ice cream)

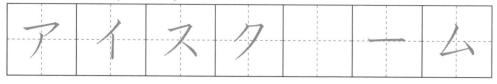

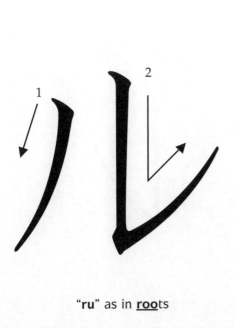

"ru" as in **roo**ts

tree **roo**ts

Writing Tip "ru" has two strokes and both are brushes.

Trace these characters.

Write the character in the boxes below, and then circle the one you think is best.

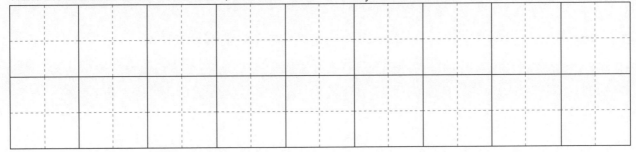

1. **ho te ru** (hotel)

2. **mi ru ku** ((cow's) mik)

3. **a ru mi ho i ru** (aluminum foil)

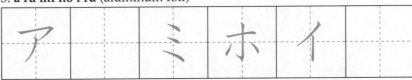

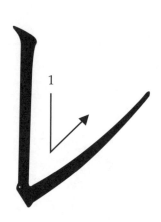

"**re**" as in <u>ra</u>in

splashing <u>ra</u>indrops

Writing Tip "**re**" has one stroke: a brush.

Trace these characters.

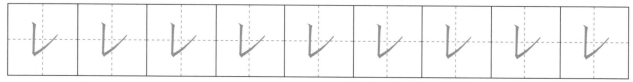

Write the character in the boxes below, and then circle the one you think is best.

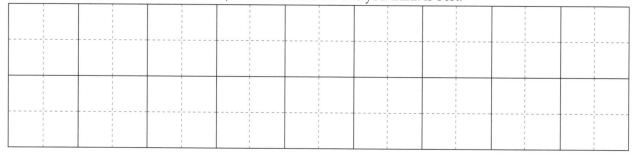

1. **re su to ra n** (restaurant)

2. **re shi i to** (receipt)

3. **e re ki** (electric guitar)

4. **ka rē ra i su** (curry rice)

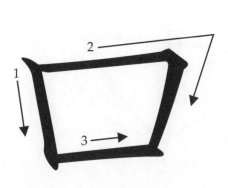

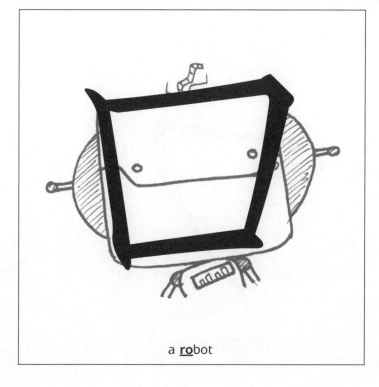

"**ro**" as in **ro**bot   a **ro**bot

Writing Tip "**ro**" has three strokes and all three are stops.

Trace these characters.

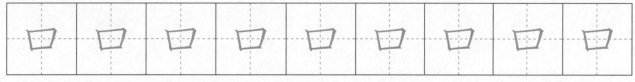

Write the character in the boxes below, and then circle the one you think is best.

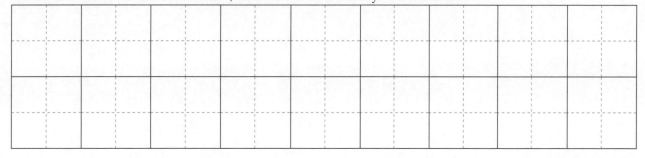

1. **ki ro** (kilogram; kilometer)   2. **su to rō** (drinking straw)

3. **te ro** (terrorism)   4. **ro shi a** (Russia)

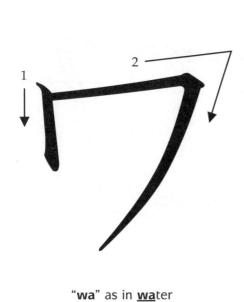

"wa" as in **wa**ter

"I **wa**nt a cookie!"

Writing Tip "wa" has two strokes: 1) a stop and 2) brush.

Trace these characters.

Write the character in the boxes below, and then circle the one you think is best.

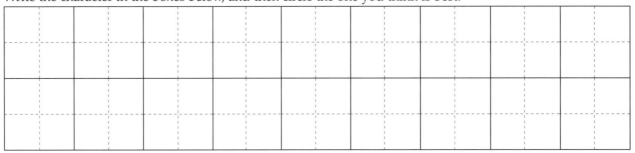

1. **ha wa i** (Hawaii)

2. **wa i ya re su** (wireless)

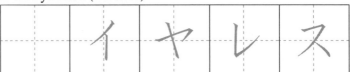

3. **wā ku shi i to** (worksheet)

"**o**" as in <u>o</u>ak
(same pronunciation as オ)

"<u>**Oh**</u>, this cookie is <u>*oishii*</u> (delicious)!"

Writing Tip "o" has two strokes: 1) a brush and 2) stop.

Trace these characters.

Write the character in the boxes below, and then circle the one you think is best.

As a grammatical object marker, ヲ "o" is rarely used to write sentences, except in telegrams and some video games. Trace the light grey characters and write the character by yourself.

su tā to bo ta n o   o shi te ku da sa i (Push the start button.)

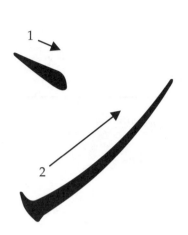

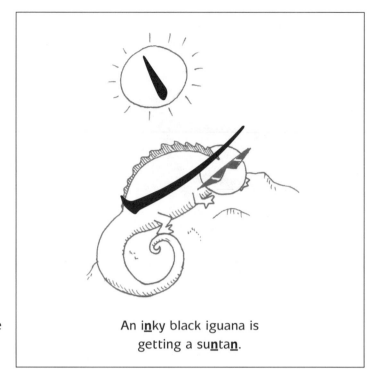

"n" as in i**n**k
(pronounced by touching the back of the
tongue to the roof of the mouth)

An i**n**ky black iguana is
getting a su**n**ta**n**.

Writing Tip "**n**" has two strokes: 1) a stop and 2) brush. (Note: ン "**n**" and ソ "**so**" look similar. A big difference is that "**n**" is written more from left to right, and "**so**" is written more from top to bottom.)

Trace these characters.

Write the character in the boxes below, and then circle the one you think is best.

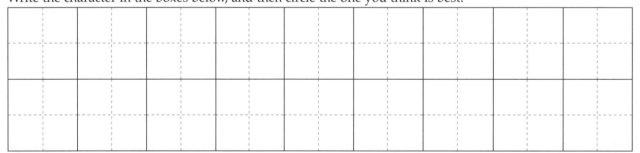

1. **me ro n** (melon)

2. **ma ra so n** (any running race)

3. **rā me n** (ramen noodles)

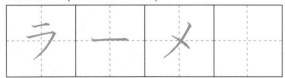

4. **mi shi n** (sewing machine)

READING PRACTICE 3: マ ～ ン

You should be able to read the words below now. Cover the right hand side of the page so you can only see the hiragana words on the left. Try reading them aloud, and then check with the romaji on the right hand side. Keep practicing until you can read them all. For an extra challenge try saying the English words before you check.

Katakana	Romaji (English)
ト マ ト	**to ma to** (tomato)
マ イ ク	**ma i ku** (microphone)
ミ キ サ ー	**mi ki sā** (blender)
チ ー ム	**chi i mu** (team)
ホ ー ム ス テ イ	**hō mu su te i** (home stay)
ア ニ メ	**a ni me** (Japanese cartoons)
シ ナ モ ン	**shi na mo n** (cinnamon)
モ ニ タ ー	**mo ni tā** (monitor)
タ イ ヤ	**ta i ya** (tire)
イ ヤ ホ ン	**i ya ho n** (earphones)
ユ ー モ ア	**yū mo a** (humor)
ク レ ヨ ン	**ku re yo n** (crayon)
ヨ ー ヨ ー	**yō yō** (yo-yo)
カ メ ラ	**ka me ra** (camera)
ク ラ ス	**ku ra su** (school class)
ア イ ス ク リ ー ム	**a i su ku ri i mu** (ice cream)
ホ テ ル	**ho te ru** (hotel)
ミ ル ク	**mi ru ku** (cow's milk)
レ ス ト ラ ン	**re su to ran** (restaurant)
レ シ ー ト	**re shi i to** (receipt)
ス ト ロ ー	**su to rō** (drinking straw)
キ ロ	**ki ro** (kilogram; kilometer)
ワ ー ク シ ー ト	**wā ku shi i to** (worksheet)
ワ イ ヤ レ ス	**wa i ya re su** (wireless)
メ ロ ン	**me ro n** (melon)
ラ ー メ ン	**rā me n** (ramen noodles)
ミ シ ン	**mi shi n** (sewing machine)
マ ラ ソ ン	**ma ra so n** (any running race)

Romaji pronunciation guide:

a as in father and bother

i as in Hawaii and beat

u as in glue and youth

e as in red and bed

o as in oak and bone

SECTION TWO
Katakana Usage Rules

Katakana has a few basic rules to keep in mind. This section introduces the four katakana rules with simple explanations and many useful example words. Pay close attention to these example words; they will illustrate the rules and make them easier to understand and remember.

Although some of the rules are the same as hiragana, katakana has different uses than hiragana so its rules are a bit different too. First, the hiragana rule for changing the pronunciation of は, へ, and を when using them as grammatical particles does not apply to katakana since katakana characters are not used as particles (except in telegraphs, video games, and so on). Second, instead of the complicated rule for making long vowels in hiragana, you simply add a long dash ー called a **chōon** (long vowel) mark in katakana. For example, "cake" is written ケーキ (**kē ki**) with a **chōon** mark after the ケ (**ke**).

Katakana has one new rule that describes how to make 33 additional syllables for writing foreign words (see Rule 4). As you master the four rules of katakana usage you will be able to write any katakana word you like. After this chapter all you will need is practice, and you will be a proficient reader and writer of katakana.

RULE 1   TENTEN (˝) AND MARU (°)

The first katakana rule describes how certain characters change pronunciations when the marks called **tenten** (˝) and **maru** (°) are added to them. There are 18 characters that take the tenten (˝) mark, and there are 5 characters that take the maru (°) mark. The chart below summarizes the changes when these marks are added.

23 Tenten and Maru Characters

ガ ga	ギ gi	グ gu	ゲ ge	ゴ go
ザ za	ジ ji	ズ zu	ゼ ze	ゾ zo
ダ da			デ de	ド do
バ ba	ビ bi	ブ bu	ベ be	ボ bo
パ pa	ピ pi	プ pu	ペ pe	ポ po

Trace the grey characters and marks, and try writing them on your own in the blank boxes.

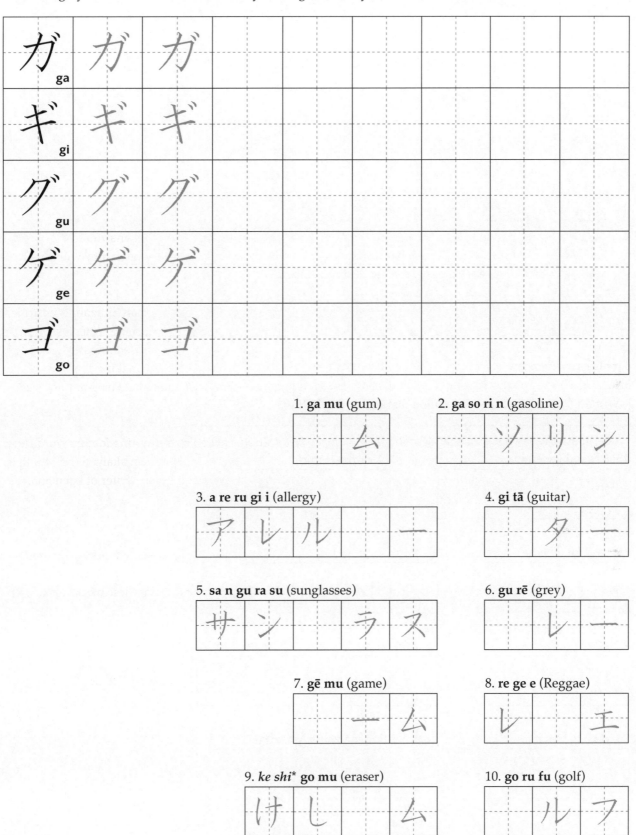

1. ga mu (gum)

2. ga so ri n (gasoline)

3. a re ru gi i (allergy)

4. gi tā (guitar)

5. sa n gu ra su (sunglasses)

6. gu rē (grey)

7. gē mu (game)

8. re ge e (Reggae)

9. *ke shi** go mu (eraser)

10. go ru fu (golf)

*hiragana

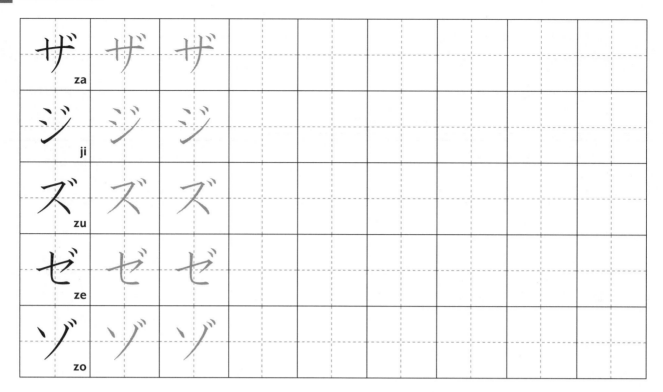

11. **ra za ni a** (lasagna)

12. **rē zā** (laser)

13. **o re n ji** (orange)

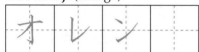

14. **ra ji o** (radio)

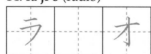

15. **chi i zu** (cheese)

16. **ji i n zu** (jeans)

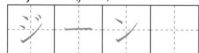

17. **gā ze** (gauze)

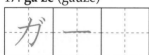

18. **zero** (zero)

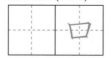

19. **ze mi** (seminar)

20. **ri zō to** (resort)

21. **a ma zo n** (Amazon)

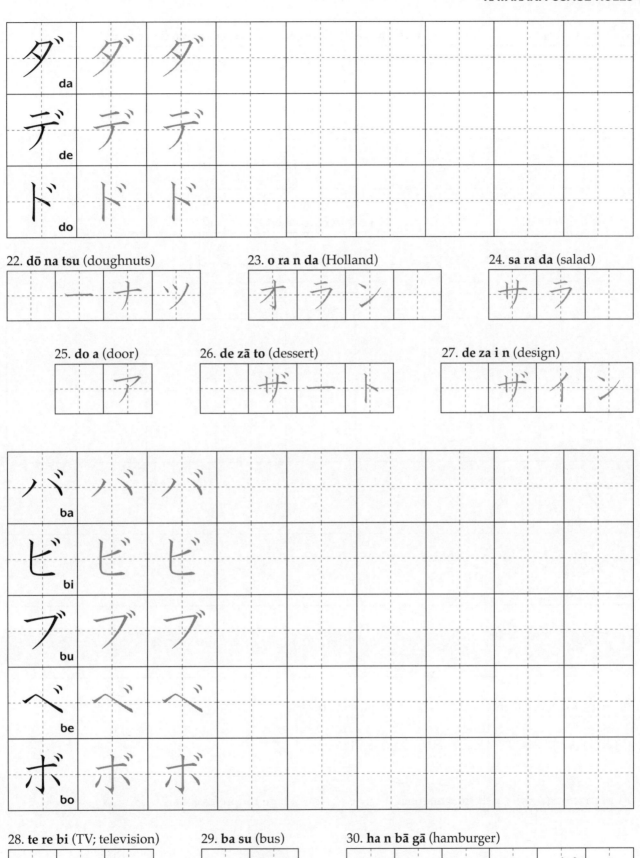

ダ da ダ ダ

デ de デ デ

ド do ド ド

22. dō na tsu (doughnuts)

ー ナ ツ

23. o ra n da (Holland)

オ ラ ン

24. sa ra da (salad)

サ ラ

25. do a (door)

ア

26. de zā to (dessert)

ザ ー ト

27. de za i n (design)

ザ イ ン

バ ba バ バ

ビ bi ビ ビ

ブ bu ブ ブ

ベ be ベ ベ

ボ bo ボ ボ

28. te re bi (TV; television)

テ レ

29. ba su (bus)

ス

30. ha n bā gā (hamburger)

ハ ン ー ガ ー

31. **be ru to** (belt)

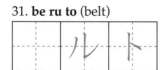

32. **zu bo n** (pants; trousers)

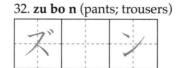

33. **ki i bō do** (keyboard)

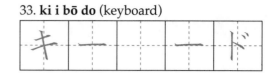

34. **bu ra ji ru** (Brazil)

35. **tē bu ru** (table)

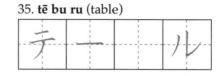

36. **i be n to** (event)

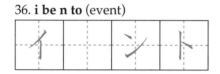

37. **ko n bi ni** (convenience store)

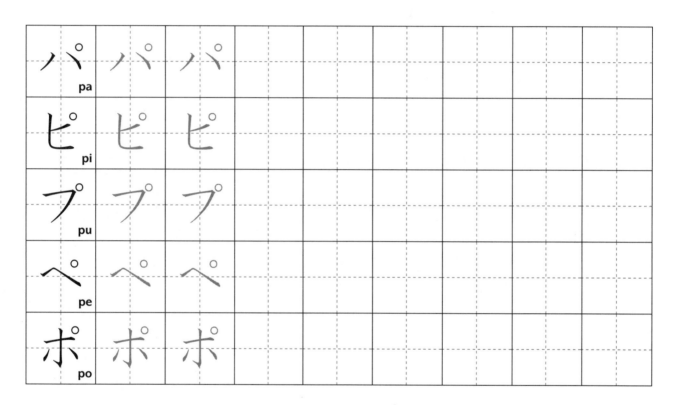

38. **de pā to** (department store)

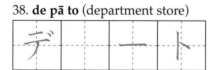

39. **pa su ta** (pasta)

40. **pi za** (pizza)

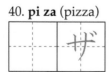

41. **pi a no** (piano)

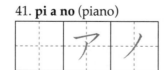

42. **pu ro** (professional)

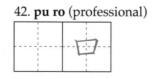

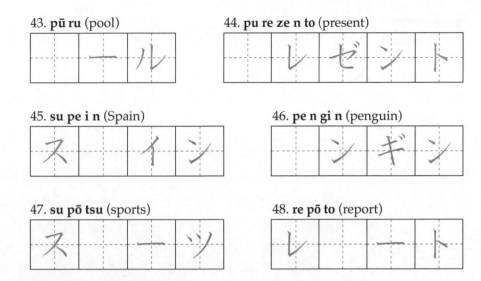

43. **pū ru** (pool)

44. **pu re ze n to** (present)

45. **su pe i n** (Spain)

46. **pe n gi n** (penguin)

47. **su pō tsu** (sports)

48. **re pō to** (report)

READING PRACTICE 4: TENTEN AND MARU

You should be able to read the words below now. Try covering the answers on the right hand side and reading the katakana words on the left. Try to guess the English meaning of each word before looking at the answers.

ガ ム	**ga mu** (gum)
ギ タ ー	**gi tā** (guitar)
サ ン グ ラ ス	**sa n gu ra su** (sunglasses)
ゲ ー ム	**gē mu** (game)
ゴ ル フ	**go ru fu** (golf)
ラ ザ ニ ア	**ra za ni a** (lasagna)
チ ー ズ	**chi i zu** (cheese)
ゼ ロ	**ze ro** (zero)
リ ゾ ー ト	**ri zō to** (resort)
サ ラ ダ	**sa ra da** (salad)
デ ザ ー ト	**de zā to** (dessert)
ド ア	**do a** (door)
バ ス	**ba su** (bus)
テ レ ビ	**te re bi** (TV; television)
テ ー ブ ル	**tē bu ru** (table)
ベ ル ト	**be ru to** (belt)
キ ー ボ ー ド	**ki i bō do** (keyboard)
パ ス タ	**pa su ta** (pasta)
ピ ア ノ	**pi a no** (piano)
プ ー ル	**pū ru** (pool)
ス ペ イ ン	**su pe i n** (Spain)
ス ポ ー ツ	**su pō tsu** (sports)

RULE 2 COMBINED CHARACTERS

There are three special katakana characters that are used extensively in combination with 11 consonants to form 33 additional sounds. When combined in this way "**ya**," "**yu**" and "**yo**" are written in half-size characters at the bottom left corner, as in the examples below. The chart below illustrates these 33 blended sounds, called **yǒ'on**.

33 Combined Characters

キャ	キュ	キョ
kya	kyu	kyo
シャ	シュ	ショ
sha	shu	sho
チャ	チュ	チョ
cha	chu	cho
ニャ	ニュ	ニョ
nya	nyu	nyo
ヒャ	ヒュ	ヒョ
hya	hyu	hyo

ギャ	ギュ	ギョ
gya	gyu	gyo
ジャ	ジュ	ジョ
ja	ju	jo

ミャ	ミュ	ミョ
mya	myu	myo
リャ	リュ	リョ
rya	ryu	ryo

ビャ	ビュ	ビョ
bya	byu	byo
ピャ	ピュ	ピョ
pya	pyu	pyo

Trace the light grey characters, and then try to complete the example words with the correct combined characters.

kya

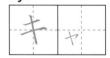

kyu

kyo*

***kyo** キョ is only used in less common words, which are not included here.

1. **kya n pu** (camp)

2. **su kya nā** (scanner)

3. **bā be kyū** (barbecue)

バ	ー	ベ			ー

gya		**gyu**		**gyo**	
ギ	ャ	ギ	ュ	ギ	ョ

4. **gya ra ri i** (gallery)

		ラ	リ	ー

5. **gya n bu ru** (to gamble; gambling)

		ン	ブ	ル

6. **re gyu rā** (regular (gasoline))

レ			ラ	ー

7. **gyō za** (pot stickers)

		ー	ザ

sha		**shu**		**sho**	
シ	ャ	シ	ュ	シ	ョ

8. **shā pe n** (mechanical pencil (sharp + pencil))

		ー	ペ	ン

9. **sha wā** (shower)

		ワ	ー

10. **shū zu** (shoes)

		ー	ズ

11. **rō sho n** (lotion)

ロ	ー		ン

ja		**ju**		**jo**	
ジ	ャ	ジ	ュ	ジ	ョ

12. **ja mu** (jam)

		ム

13. **jo gi n gu** (jogging)

		ギ	ン	グ

14. **jū su** (juice)

15. **pa ja ma** (pajama)

cha

chu

cho

16. **cha n ne ru** (channel)

17. **shi chū** (stew)

18. **cho ko rē to** (chocolate)

19. **chō ku** (chalk)

nya*

nyu

nyo*

***nya** ニャ and **nyo** ニョ are only used in less common words, which are not included here.

20. **me nyū** (menu)

21. **nyū su** (news)

hya*

hyu*

hyo*

*These character combinations are only used in less common words, which are not included here.

bya*

byu

byo*

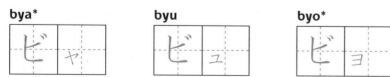

***bya** ビャ and **byo** ビョ are only used in less common words, which are not included here.

22. **i n ta byū** (interview)

| イ | ン | タ | | | ー |

23. **re byū** (review)

| レ | | | ー |

pya*

| ピ | ャ |

pyu

| ピ | ュ |

pyo*

| ピ | ョ |

***pya** ピャ and **pyo** ビョ are only used in less common words, which are not included here.

24. **ko n pyū tā** (computer)

| コ | ン | | | | ー | タ | ー |

25. **pyū ma** (puma)

| | | | ー | マ |

mya*

| ミ | ャ |

myu

| ミ | ュ |

myo*

| ミ | ョ |

***mya** ミャ and **myo** ミョ are only used in less common words, which are not included here.

26. **myū ji ka ru** (musical)

| | | | ー | ジ | カ | ル |

27. **myū to** (mute – volume)

| | | ー | ト |

rya*

| リ | ャ |

ryu

| リ | ュ |

ryo*

| リ | ョ |

***rya** リャ and **ryo** リョ are only used in less common words, which are not included here.

28. **ba ryū** (value)

| バ | | | ー |

29. **bo ryū mu** (volume)

| ボ | | | ー | ム |

READING PRACTICE 5: COMBINED CHARACTERS

You should be able to read the words below now. Try covering the answers on the right hand side and reading the katakana words on the left. Try to guess the English meaning of each word before looking at the answers.

キ ャ ン プ	**kya n pu** (to camp; camping)
ス キ ャ ナ ー	**su kya nā** (scanner)
バ ー ベ キ ュ ー	**bā be kyū** (barbecue)
ギ ャ ラ リ ー	**gya ra ri i** (gallery)
レ ギ ュ ラ ー	**re gyu rā** (regular)
ギ ョ ー ザ	**gyō za** (pot stickers)
シ ャ ワ ー	**sha wā** (shower)
シ ュ ー ズ	**shū zu** (shoes)
ロ ー シ ョ ン	**rō sho n** (lotion)
ジ ャ ム	**ja mu** (jam)
ジ ャ ズ	**ja zu** (jazz)
ジ ュ ー ス	**jū su** (juice)
ジ ョ ギ ン グ	**jo gi n gu** (jogging)
チ ャ ン ネ ル	**cha n ne ru** (channel)
シ チ ュ ー	**shi chū** (stew)
チ ョ コ レ ー ト	**cho ko rē to** (chocolate)
チ ョ ー ク	**chō ku** (chalk)
メ ニ ュ ー	**me nyū** (menu)
ニ ュ ー ス	**nyū su** (news)
イ ン タ ビ ュ ー	**i n ta byū** (interview)
コ ン ピ ュ ー タ ー	**ko n pyū tā** (computer)
ミ ュ ー ジ カ ル	**myū ji ka ru** (musical)
バ リ ュ ー	**ba ryū** (value)

RULE 3 SMALL "TSU" (ッ)

A small "TSU" (ッ) is pronounced as a short, silent pause. In romaji it is usually indicated by doubling the following consonant (see examples below). Small "tsu" is written in the bottom left hand corner, like small "ya," "yu" and "yo." Complete the example words by tracing the light grey characters and writing a small "tsu" in the appropriate area of the blank boxes.

Example of regular-sized "**tsu**" Example of small "**tsu**"

1. **ba ggu** (bag)

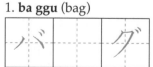

2. **so kku su** (socks)

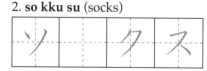

3. **pi ku ni kku** (picnic)

4. **sa kkā** (soccer)

5. **sa n do i cchi** (sandwich)

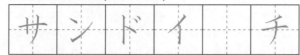

6. **ki cchi n** (kitchen)

7. **ho tto do ggu** (hotdog)

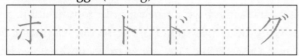

8. **chi ke tto** (ticket)

9. **pa i na ppu ru** (pineapple)

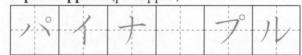

10. **ka ppu** (cup)

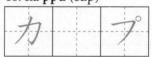

READING PRACTICE 6: SMALL "tsu" (ツ)

You should be able to read the words below now. Try covering the answers on the right hand side and reading the katakana words on the left. Remember that a small "**tsu**" ツ is read as a short, silent pause. Try to guess the English meaning of each word before looking at the answers.

ジャケット ト	**ja ke tto** (jacket)
バッグ	**ba ggu** (bag)
サンドイッチ	**san n do i cchi** (sandwich)
カップ	**ka ppu** (cup)
コッップ	**ko ppu** (drinking glass)
キッチン	**ki cchi n** (kitchen)
ベッド	**be ddo** (bed)
クローゼット	**ku rō ze tto** (closet)
カセットテープ	**ka se tto tē pu** (cassette tape)
ペット	**pe tto** (pet)
サッカー	**sa kkā** (soccer)
クリップ	**ku ri ppu** (paper clip)
スケッチ	**su ke cchi** (sketch)
キット	**ki tto** (kit)
セット	**se tto** (set)
ダイエット	**da i e tto** (diet)
ポテトチップ	**po te to chi ppu** (potato chips)
クラシック	**ku ra shi kku** (classic)
コック	**ko kku** (cook)
ロッカー	**ro kkā** (locker)
ネックレス	**ne kku re su** (necklace)

キャッチボール　　kya cchi bō ru (playing catch)
ブレースレット　　bu rē su re tto (bracelet)

RULE 4 ADDITIONAL COMBINED CHARACTERS

As Japan has become more international, the need to better approximate the foreign names and words from various countries around the world has increased. In 1991 the Japanese government adopted an official list of 32 additional character combinations, and one new character "**vu**" ヴ, for the express purpose of writing foreign words. It also clarified that other additional combinations, as needed, may be used.

You may occasionally see new character combinations as you read books, magazines and web pages. Don't be alarmed, all character combinations follow the same basic principles of pronunciation: the first character indicates the initial sound and it combines with the whole sound of the second character. For example, トゥ takes the initials sound "**t**" and the final sound "**u**" to make "**tu**." Since many of the new character combinations are used to write words of foreign languages other than English, and because these words are uncommon in Japanese, the character combination will be introduced, but the unusual examples will not.

ye*

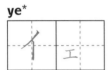

*****ye** イェ is only used in less common words, which are not included here.

wi

1. **ha ro wi i n** (Halloween)

we

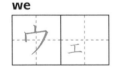

2. **we bu** (world wide web)

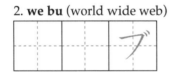

3. **ku wē to** (Kuwait)

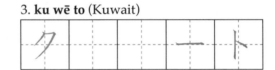

wo

4. **su to ppu wo cchi** (stopwatch)

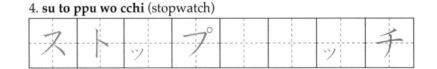

va

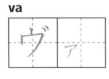

5. **va i o ri n** (violin, also written バイオリン **ba i o ri n**)

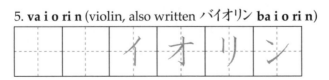

vi

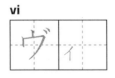

6. **vi sa** (visa, also ビサ **bi sa**)

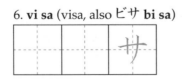

vu*

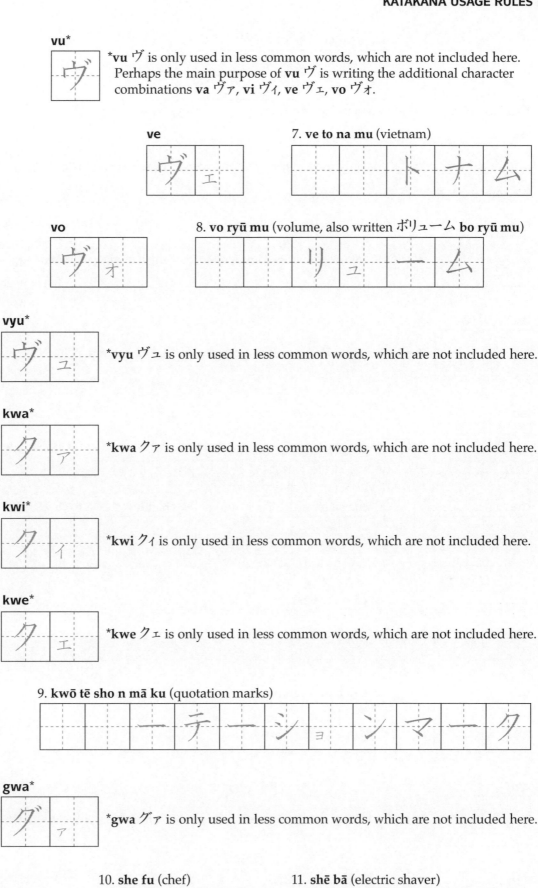

*vu ヴ is only used in less common words, which are not included here. Perhaps the main purpose of **vu** ヴ is writing the additional character combinations **va** ヴァ, **vi** ヴィ, **ve** ヴェ, **vo** ヴォ.

ve

7. ve to na mu (vietnam)

vo

8. vo ryū mu (volume, also written ボリューム **bo ryū mu**)

vyu*

*vyu ヴュ is only used in less common words, which are not included here.

kwa*

*kwa クァ is only used in less common words, which are not included here.

kwi*

*kwi クィ is only used in less common words, which are not included here.

kwe*

*kwe クェ is only used in less common words, which are not included here.

kwo

9. kwō tē sho n mā ku (quotation marks)

gwa*

*gwa グァ is only used in less common words, which are not included here.

she

10. she fu (chef)

11. shē bā (electric shaver)

je

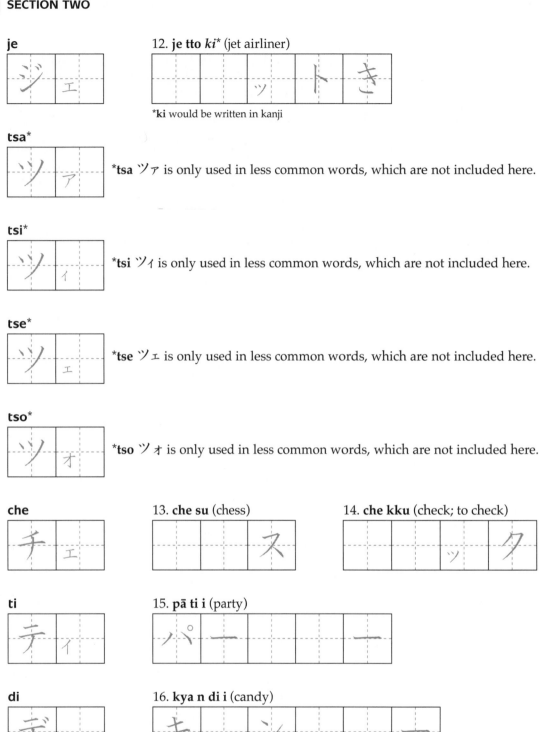

12. je tto *ki* (jet airliner)

*****ki** would be written in kanji

tsa*

*****tsa** ツァ is only used in less common words, which are not included here.

tsi*

*****tsi** ツィ is only used in less common words, which are not included here.

tse*

*****tse** ツェ is only used in less common words, which are not included here.

tso*

*****tso** ツォ is only used in less common words, which are not included here.

che

13. che su (chess)

14. che kku (check; to check)

ti

15. pā ti i (party)

di

16. kya n di i (candy)

tyu*

*****tyu** テュ is only used in less common words, which are not included here.

dyu

17. dyu e tto (duet)

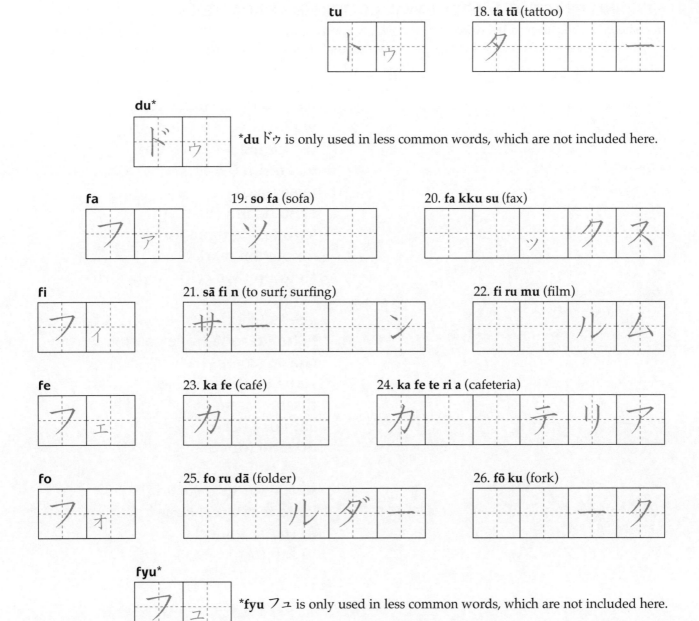

tu

18. ta tū (tattoo)

du*

***du** ドゥ is only used in less common words, which are not included here.

fa

19. so fa (sofa)

20. fa kku su (fax)

fi

21. sā fi n (to surf; surfing)

22. fi ru mu (film)

fe

23. ka fe (café)

24. ka fe te ri a (cafeteria)

fo

25. fo ru dā (folder)

26. fō ku (fork)

fyu*

***fyu** フュ is only used in less common words, which are not included here.

READING PRACTICE 7: ADDITIONAL COMBINED CHARACTERS

You should be able to read the words below now. Try covering the answers on the right hand side and reading the katakana words on the left. Try to guess the English meaning of each word before looking at the answers.

ハ ロ ウ ィ ー ン	**ha ro wi i n** (Halloween)
ウ ェ ブ	**we bu** (world wide web)
ウ ォ ー ク マ ン	**wō ku ma n** (walkman)
ヴ ァ イ オ リ ン	**va i o ri n** (violin)
ヴ ィ サ	**vi sa** (visa)
ヴ ェ ト ナ ム	**ve to na mu** (Vietnam)
ク ォ ー テ ー シ ョ ン マ ー ク	**kwō te sho n mā ku** (quotation marks)
ス ト ッ プ ウ ォ ッ チ	**su to ppu wo cchi** (stopwatch)
タ ト ゥ ー	**ta tū** (tatto)
シ ェ フ	**she fu** (chef)
ジ ェ ッ ト コ ー ス タ ー	**je tto kō su tā** (rollercoaster)
チ ェ ス	**che su** (chess)
ス パ ゲ ッ テ ィ	**su pa ge tti** (spaghetti)
テ ィ ッ シ ュ	**ti sshu** (tissue)
シ ー デ ィ ー	**shi i di i** (CD)
デ ュ エ ッ ト	**du e tto** (duet)
ソ フ ァ	**so fa** (sofa)
サ ー フ ィ ン	**sā fi n** (to surf; surfing)
カ フ ェ テ リ ア	**ka fe te ri a** (cafeteria)
フ ォ ル ダ ー	**fo ru dā** (folder)
フ ォ ー ク	**fō ku** (fork)

SECTION THREE
Reading and Writing Practice

Commonly Mistaken Katakana

Commonly Mistaken Combined Characters

In My Home

Family Restaurant (Food, Part A)

Picnic Lunch (Food, Part B)

Computers and Technology

Sports and Athletics

Sound Symbolic Words

World Map: Africa

World Map: Asia and the Middle East

World Map: Europe

World Map: North and South America

World Map: Oceania

なまえ _____

Commonly Mistaken Katakana

Part A:	Part B:
Circle the correct katakana character.	Circle the correct katakana character.

	Part A		Part B
a	マ ワ ヤ ⓐ ケ ヌ フ	**ho**	ハ オ モ ネ ⓗ サ ナ
1. **ko**	ヒ コ ロ ヨ ク タ ワ	1. **no**	タ ク メ ノ ナ ソ ン
2. **na**	ト ノ イ ネ キ ナ メ	2. **mu**	マ ヒ モ ス ワ ム フ
3. **nu**	タ ノ ナ ヌ メ ク ケ	3. **ri**	ソ リ ル シ ハ ン ホ
4. **su**	ヌ ネ ス ク タ メ ヲ	4. **mo**	ヒ セ ニ ミ シ サ モ
5. **tsu**	シ ソ ン リ ツ サ ミ	5. **ne**	フ ネ ラ ホ ハ ウ ラ
6. **so**	リ ン シ ツ サ メ ソ	6. **ha**	ル リ ハ ソ ホ ニ ム
7. **te**	ニ テ チ メ ヲ ナ ミ	7. **yo**	コ ユ ヲ ラ ヨ ワ ニ
8. **u**	ク ワ ヌ フ ラ ウ ヲ	8. **ro**	コ ヒ モ ロ ヨ ニ エ
9. **ku**	ケ ヲ ク ウ タ ヲ ワ	9. **ya**	ヤ カ マ メ ム メ ヌ
10. **ni**	テ ニ ユ ナ ヲ ミ ヨ	10. **me**	ノ ナ メ ヌ タ ク ケ
11. **to**	ナ イ ノ リ テ オ ト	11. **hi**	エ セ ム ヨ コ モ ヒ
12. **shi**	ツ ソ ン シ リ サ レ	12. **ru**	レ リ ル ハ ニ ノ ナ
13. **chi**	テ オ チ イ ホ ナ ム	13. **ma**	ム ア ウ マ ヌ メ ク
14. **ke**	ケ ワ フ ク タ ヲ マ	14. **mi**	ニ ミ ツ ン ソ キ シ
15. **sa**	リ シ ツ ン ソ サ ル	15. **ra**	テ ラ ウ モ フ ワ ヲ
16. **ka**	ヤ フ ラ カ タ ク ケ	16. **fu**	ク ワ ヲ ケ フ タ ナ
17. **ta**	タ ヌ ク ワ ヲ ラ メ	17. **yu**	コ ヨ ラ ワ ニ ヲ ユ

Time _____:_____   Time _____:_____

なまえ _____

Commonly Mistaken Combined Characters

Part A:
Circle the correct combined character.

Part B:
Circle the correct combined character.

ju	シュ	ジョ	(ジュ)	ショ		**di***	ティ	テュ	デュ	(ディ)
1. **gya**	ギャ	キャ	ギュ	キュ		1. **wi**	ヴィ	ウィ	ウェ	ウォ
2. **sha**	シュ	ショ	ジョ	シャ		2. **du***	トゥ	テュ	ドゥ	デュ
3. **nyo**	ミョ	ニョ	ニャ	ミュ		3. **fo**	フィ	フェ	ファ	フォ
4. **myu**	ミョ	ニュ	ミュ	ミャ		4. **vo**	ヴォ	ウォ	ヴュ	ヴィ
5. **jo**	ショ	ジュ	シュ	ジョ		5. **qwo***	グォ	クァ	クォ	クィ
6. **pyu**	ピャ	ピュ	ヒュ	ピョ		6. **va**	ウィ	ヴァ	ヴェ	ヴィ
7. **kyo**	キャ	ギャ	キョ	ギョ		7. **ti***	ディ	デュ	テュ	ティ
8. **chu**	チャ	チュ	ショ	シュ		8. **tu***	ドゥ	トゥ	テュ	ティ
9. **bya**	ビャ	ヒャ	ピャ	ビュ		9. **je**	ジェ	シェ	チェ	クェ
10. **hya**	ヒュ	ヒャ	ピャ	ビャ		10. **qwa***	ジャ	ファ	ツァ	クァ
11. **ryo**	リュ	ジュ	ニョ	リョ		11. **ve**	ウェ	ヴェ	クェ	シェ
12. **kya**	ギャ	キュ	キャ	ギョ		12. **gwa***	クァ	ファ	グァ	ヴァ
13. **byo**	ピョ	ヒュ	ビョ	ヒョ		13. **ye**	クェ	イェ	ヴェ	ツェ
14. **gyo**	キョ	ギュ	ギャ	ギョ		14. **dyu***	デュ	ヴュ	ツァ	ツォ
15. **ryu**	リュ	リョ	ニュ	リャ		15. **che**	ウェ	フェ	チェ	ヴェ

*These spellings indicate the pronunciation. When typing, however, the "x" key is used to type small characters, rather than using these spellings.

Time _____:_____

Time _____:_____

なまえ _____

In My Home

Part A: Label the places in this home with katakana characters.

| 1. bedroom (**be ddo rū mu**) | 2. shower (**sha wā**) | 3. toilet, restroom (**to i re**) |
| 4. living room (**ri bi n gu rū mu**) | 5. dining room (**da i ni n gu rū mu**) | 6. kitchen (**ki cchi n**) |

Part B: Complete the sentences below by describing where each household item is located.

1. The blender (**mi ki sā**) is in the kitchen.

<u>ミキサー</u>は　<u>キッチン</u>に　あります 。

2. The sofa (**so fa**) is in the living room.

_____ 。

3. The slippers (**su ri ppā**) are in the restroom.

_____ 。

4. The microwave (*de n shi** **re n ji**) is in the kitchen.

<u>でんし</u>　は　_____　に　あります 。

5. The sewing machine (**mi shi n**) is in the closet (**ku rō ze tto**).

_____ 。

6. The desk lamp (*de n ki** **su ta n do**) is in the bedroom.

でんき _____ 。

7. The table (**tē bu ru**) is in the dining room.

_____ 。

8. The iron (**a i ro n**) is in the closet (**ku rō ze tto**).

_____ 。

*hiragana

なまえ _____

Family Restaurant (Food, Part A)

menu (**me nyū**)

1. sandwich (**sa n do i cchi**)

¥400

2. cheese pizza (**chi i zu pi za**)

¥400

3. hamburger (**ha n bā gā**)

¥450

4. hotdog (**ho tto do ggu**)

¥350

5. spaghetti (**su pa ge tti**)

¥550

6. ramen noodles (**rā me n**)

¥400

7. curry rice (**ka rē ra i su**)

¥550

8. hamburger steak (**ha n bā gu**)

¥750

9. steak (**su tē ki**)

¥950

10. French fries (**po te to fu ra i**)

¥350

11. salad (**sa ra da**)

¥400

12. soup (**sū pu**)

¥350

13. melon soda float (**ku ri i mu sō da**)

¥400

14. tomato juice (**to ma to jū su**)

¥300

15. orange juice (**o re n ji jū su**)

¥300

16. cola (**kō ra**)

¥350

17. milk (**mi ru ku**)

¥300

18. coffee (**kō hi i**)

¥350

19. ice tea (**a i su ti i**)

¥350

20. pudding (**pu ri n**)

¥350

21. ice cream (**a i su ku ri i mu**)

¥350

22. sherbet (**shā be tto**)

¥350

23. cheese cake (**chi i zu kē ki**)

¥400

Picnic Lunch (Food, Part B)

なまえ _____

Taro has almost finished packing a picnic lunch.
He wants a few more fruits, snacks, utensils and condiments.
Write in katakana below the choices he could consider.

1. oranges (**o re n ji**)

2. bananas (**ba na na**)

3. melon (**me ro n**)

4. pineapple (**pa i na ppu ru**)

5. mango (**ma n gō**)

6. kiwi fruit (**ki u i fu rū tsu**)

7. grapefruit (**gu rē pu fu rū tsu**)

8. cherries (**che ri i**)

9. olives (**o ri i bu**)

10. avocado (**a bo ka do**)

11. tomato (**to ma to**)

12. lettuce (**re ta su**)

13. celery (**se ro ri**)

14. peanuts (**pi i na ttsu**)

15. potato chips (**po te to chi ppu su**)

16. cookies (**ku kki i**)

17. crackers (**ku ra kkā**)

18. candy (**kya n di i**)

19. chocolate (**cho ko rē to**)

20. gum (**ga mu**)

21. popsicles (**a i su kya n di i**)

22. cheese (**chi i zu**)

23. yogurt (**yō gu ru to**)

24. salad dressing (**do re sshi n gu**)

25. ketchup (**ke cha ppu**)

なまえ _____

Computers and Technology

1. computer (**ko n pyū tā**)

2. personal computer (**pa so ko n**)

3. notebook computer (**nō to pa so ko n**)

4. mouse (**ma u su**)

5. keyboard (**ki i bō do**)

6. monitor (**mo ni tā**)

7. printer (**pu ri n tā**)

8. software (**so fu to**)*

9. modem (**mo de mu**)

10. web (**we bu**)

11. internet (**i n tā ne tto**)

12. home page (**hō mu pē ji**)

13. email (**mē ru**)*

14. camera (**ka me ra**)

15. digital camera (**de ji ka me**)*

16. video camera (**bi de o ka me ra**)

17. lens (**re n zu**)

18. film (**fi ru mu**)

19. TV; television (**te re bi**)

20. remote control (**ri mo ko n**)

21. video tape (**bi de o tē pu**)

22. DVD player (**DVD pu rē yā**)

D	V	D				

23. MP3 player (**MP3 pu rē yā**)

M	P	3				

24. earphones (**i ya ho n**)

25. radio (**ra ji o**)

26. cell phone (**kē ta i**)**

* Although commonly abbreviated, "software" is also written ソフトウェア (**so fu to we a**); "email" is also 電子メール (**de n shi mē ru**) or イーメール (**i i mē ru**); "digital camera" is also デジタルカメラ (**de ji ta ru ka me ra**).

** "Cell phone" is commonly written in katakana, but is still officially written in kanji 携帯電話 (**ke i ta i de n wa**).

Sports and Athletics

なまえ _____

1. sports (**su pō tsu**)

2. Olympics (**o ri n pi kku**)

3. basketball (**ba su ke tto bō ru**)

4. volleyball (**ba rē bō ru**)

5. golf (**go ru fu**)

6. football (**a me fu to**)*

7. lacosse (**ra ku ro su**)

8. tennis (**te ni su**)

9. rugby (**ra gu bi i**)

10. soccer (**sa kkā**)

11. score (**su ko a**)

12. goal (**gō ru**)

13. team (**chi i mu**)

14. uniform (**yu ni fō mu**)

15. skiing (**su ki i**)

16. snowboarding (**su nō bō do**)

17. ice skating (**a i su su kē to**)

18. ice hockey (**a i su ho kkē**)

19. surfing (**sā fi n**)

20. diving (**da i bi n gu**)

21. skateboarding (**su ke bō**)*

22. wrestling (**re su ri n gu**)

23. boxing (**bo ku shi n gu**)

24. taekwondo (**te ko n dō**)

25. marathon (**ma ra so n**)

* Although commonly abbreviated, "(American) football" is also written アメリカンフットボール (**a me ri ka n fu tto bō ru**); "skateboarding" is also written スケートボード (**su kē to bō do**)

なまえ ＿＿＿＿＿＿＿＿

Sound Symbolic Words

General Sounds

1. The rain is pouring down.
   あめが（　　）ふっている。　　**(zā zā)**

2. The wind is howling.
   かぜが（　　）と　ふいている。　　**(hyū hyū)**

3. The phone is ringing.
   でんわが（　　）と　なっている。　　**(ri i n)**

4. The microwave timer rang.
   でんしレンジが（　　）と　なった。　　**(chi n)**

5. The children made a lot of noise
   こどもが（　　）さわいだ。　　**(wa i wa i)**

Animal Sounds

6. Dogs say "Woof! Woof!"
   いぬは（　　）と　なく。　　**(wan wan)**

7. Cats say "meow."
   ねこは（　　）と　なく。　　**(nyā)**

8. Crows say "kah kah."
   カラスは（　　）と　なく。　　**(kā kā)**

9. Frogs say "ribit."
   かえるは（　　）と　なく。　　**(ke ro ke ro)**

10. Mice say "squeak!"
    ねずみは（　　）と　なく。　　**(chū chū)**

11. Roosters say "cock-a-doodle-doo!"
    にわとりは（　　）と　なく。　　**(ko ke ko kkō)**

Psychological States

12. I'm excited (nervous/anxious; lit. my heart is pounding).
    むねが（　　）する。　　**(do ki do ki)**

13. I'm excited (positive sense; lit. my heart is fluttering).
    むねが（　　）する。　　**(wa ku wa ku)**

World Map: Africa

なまえ ＿＿＿＿＿＿＿＿＿＿

1. Algeria (**a ru je ri a**)

2. Angola (**a n go ra**)

3. Uganda (**u ga n da**)

4. Egypt (**e ji pu to**)

5. Ethiopia (**e chi o pi a**)

6. Eritrea (**e ri to ri a**)

7. Ghana (**gā na**)

8. Cape Verde (**kā bo be ru de**)

9. Canary Islands (**ka na ri a** *sho tō*)*
諸島

10. Gabon (**ga bo n**)

11. Cameroon (**ka me rū n**)

12. Gambia (**ga n bi a**)

13. Guinea (**gi ni a**)

14. Guinea-Bissau (**gi ni a bi sa u**)

15. Ivory Coast (**kō to ji bo wā ru**)

16. Sao Tome and Principe
(**sa n to me pu ri n shi pu**)

17. Republic of the Congo
(**ko n go** *kyō wa ko ku*)*
共和国

18. Democratic Republic
of the Congo
(**ko n go** *mi n shu kyō wa ko ku*)*
民主共和国

19. Kenya (**ke ni a**)

20. Comoros (**ko mo ro**)

21. Zambia (**za n bi a**)

22. Sierra Leone (**she ra re o ne**)

23. Djibouti (**ji bu chi**)

24. Zimbabwe (**ji n ba bu e**)

25. Sudan (**sū da n**)

26. Swaziland (**su wa ji ra n do**)

27. Seychelles (**se i she ru**)

28. Equatorial Guinea
(*se ki dō* **gi ni a**)*
赤道

29. Senegal (**se ne ga ru**)

30. Somali (**so ma ri a**)

31. Tanzania (**ta n za ni a**)

32. Chad (**cha do**)

33. Tunisia (**chu ni ji a**)

34. Togo (**tō go**)

35. Nigeria (**na i je ri a**)

36. Namibia (**na mi bi a**)

37. Niger (**ni jē ru**)

38. Central African Republic
(*chū ō* **a fu ri ka**)*
中央

39. Western Sahara
(*ni shi* **sa ha ra**)*
西

40. Burkina Faso
(**bu ru ki na fa so**)

41. Burundi (**bu ru n ji**)

42. Benin (**be na n**)

43. Botswana (**bo tsu wa na**)

44. Madagascar
(**ma da ga su ka ru**)

45. Malawi (**ma ra u i**)

46. Mali (**ma ri**)

47. Mauritius (**mō ri sha su**)

48. Mauritania
(**mō ri ta ni a**)

49. Mozambique
(**mo za n bi i ku**)

50. Morocco (**mo ro kko**)

51. Libya (**ri bi a**)

52. Liberia (**ri be ri a**)

53. Rwanda (**ru wa n da**)

54. Lesotho (**re so to**)

55. Reunion (**re yu ni o n**)

56. South Africa
(*mi na mi* **a fu ri ka**)*
南

Italic letters indicate the kanji pronunciation.

なまえ _____

World Map: Asia and the Middle East

(In Asia most country names are written in katakana, except for Japan 日本; North Korea 北朝鮮; South Korea 韓国; China 中国 and Taiwan 台湾.)

1. Cyprus (**ki pu ro su**)

2. Lebanon (**re ba no n**)

3. Palestine (**pa re su chi na**)

4. Israel (**i su ra e ru**)

5. Jordan (**yo ru da n**)

6. Mongolia (**mo n go ru**)

7. Macao (**ma ka o**)

8. Philippines (**fi ri pi n**)

9. Vietnam (**be to na mu**)

10. Laos (**ra o su**)

11. Cambodia (**ka n bo ji a**)

12. Brunei (**bu ru ne i**)

13. Malaysia (**ma rē shi a**)

14. Singapore (**shi n ga pō ru**)

15. Indonesia (**i n do ne shi a**)

16. Thailand (**ta i**)

17. Myanmar (**mya n mā**)

18. Bangladesh (**ba n gu ra de shu**)

19. Bhutan (**bū ta n**)

20. Nepal (**ne pā ru**)

21. India (**i n do**)

22. Sri Lanka (**su ri ra n ka**)

23. Maldives (**mo ru di vu**)

24. Pakistan (**pa ki su ta n**)

25. Afghanistan (**a fu ga ni su ta n**)

26. Iran (**i ra n**)

27. Tajikistan (**ta ji ki su ta n**)

28. Kyrgyz (**ki ru gi su**)

29. Kazakhstan (**ka za fu su ta n**)

30. Uzbekistan (**u zu be ki su ta n**)

31. Turkmenistan (**to ru ku me ni su ta n**)

32. Azerbaijan (**a ze ru ba i ja n**)

33. Georgia (**gu ru ji a**)

34. Turkey (**to ru ko**)

35. Armenia (**a ru me ni a**)

36. Syria (**shi ri a**)

37. Iraq (**i ra ku**)

38. Saudi Arabia (**sa u ji a ra bi a**)

39. Oman (**o mā n**)

40. Yemen (**i e me n**)

41. UAE* (**a ra bu** *shu chō koku ren pō*)

首 長 国 連 邦

* (United Arab Emirates, *italic* letters indicate the kanji pronunciation.)

なまえ _____

World Map: Europe

1. Iceland (**a i su ra n do**)

2. Ireland (**a i ru ra n do**)

3. Albania (**a ru ba ni a**)

4. Andorra (**a n do ra**)

5. England (**i gi ri su**)

6. Italy (**i ta ri a**)

7. Ukraine (**u ku ra i na**)

8. Estonia (**e su to ni a**)

9. Austria (**ō su to ri a**)

10. Holland (**o ra n da**)

11. Greece (**gi ri sha**)

12. Croatia (**ku ro a chi a**)

13. San Marino (**sa n ma ri no**)

14. Gibraltar (**gi bu ra ru ta ru**)

15. Switzerland (**su i su**)

16. Sweden (**su wē de n**)

17. Spain (**su pe i n**)

18. Slovakia (**su ro ba ki a**)

19. Slovenia (**su ro be ni a**)

20. Czech Republic (**che ko**)

21. Denmark (**de n mā ku**)

22. Germany (**do i tsu**)

23. Norway (**no ru wē**)

24. Vatican City (**ba chi ka n**) 市国

25. Hungary (**ha n ga ri i**)

26. Finland (**fi n ra n do**)

27. Faroe Islands (**fe rō *sho tō***)* 諸島

28. France (**fu ra n su**)

29. Russia (**ro shi a**)

30. Bulgaria (**bu ru ga ri a**)

31. Belarus (**be ra rū shi**)

32. Belgium (**be ru gi i**)

33. Poland (**pō ra n do**)

34. Portugal (**po ru to ga ru**)

35. Macedonia (**ma ke do ni a**)

36. Malta (**ma ru ta**)

37. Serbia and Montenegro
(**se ru bi a • mo n te ne gu ro**)

38. Monaco (**mo na ko**)

39. Moldova (**mo ru do ba**)

40. Latvia (**ra to bi a**)

41. Lithuania (**ri to a ni a**)

42. Liechtenstein
(**ri hi te n shu ta i n**)

43. Romania (**rū ma ni a**)

44. Luxembourg
(**ru ku se n bu ru ku**)

45. Bosnia and Herzegovina
(**bo su ni a • he ru tse go bi na**)

Italic letters indicate the kanji pronunciation.

なまえ _____

World Map: North and South America

1. Greenland (**gu ri i n ra n do**)

2. Canada (**ka na da**)

3. United State of America
(**a me ri ka** *ga sshū koku*)*
合　衆　国

4. Mexico (**me ki shi ko**)

5. Guatemala (**gu a te ma ra**)

6. Belize (**be ri i zu**)

7. El Salvador (**e ru sa ru ba do ru**)

8. Honduras (**ho n ju ra su**)

9. Nicaragua (**ni ka ra gu a**)

10. Costa Rica (**ko su ta ri ka**)

11. Panama
(**pa na ma**)

12. Bermuda Islands (**ba myū da**)

13. The Bahamas (**ba ha ma**)

14. Cuba (**kyū ba**)

15. Venezuela (**be ne zu e ra**)

16. Colombia (**ko ro n bi a**)

17. Ecuador (**e ku a do ru**)

18. Guyana (**ga i a na**)

19. Suriname (**su ri na mu**)

20. French Guiana (**fu ra n su** *ryō* **gi a na**)*
領

21. Peru (**pe rū**)

22. Brazil (**bu ra ji ru**)

23. Bolivia (**bo ri bi a**)

24. Paraguay (**pa ra gu a i**)

25. Chili (**chi ri**)

26. Argentina (**a ru ze n chi n**)

27. Uruguay (**u ru gu a i**)

28. Falkland Islands (**fō ku ra n do** *sho tō*)*
諸　島

Italic letters indicate the kanji pronunciation.

World Map: Oceania

なまえ _____

1. American Samoa
(**a me ri ka** *ryō* **sa mo a**)*

				領			

2. Australia (**ō su to ra ri a**)

3. Northern Mariana Islands
(*ki ta* **ma ri a na** *sho tō*)*

北				諸	島

4. Kiribati (**ki ri ba su**)

5. Guam (**gu a mu**)

6. Cook Islands (**ku kku** *sho tō*)*

			諸	島

7. Samoa (**sa mo a**)

8. Solomon Islands (**so ro mo n** *sho tō*)*

				諸	島

9. Tuvalu (**tsu ba ru**)

10. Tonga (**to n ga**)

11. Nauru (**na u ru**)

12. New Caledonia (**nyū ka re do ni a**)

13. New Zealand (**nyū ji i ra n do**)

14. Vanuatu (**ba nu a tsu**)

15. Papua New Guinea (**pa pu a nyū gi ni a**)

16. Palau (**pa ra o**)

17. Fiji (**fi ji i**)

18. Marshal Islands (**mā sha ru** *sho tō*)*

				諸	島

19. Micronesia (**mi ku ro ne shi a**)

20. French Polynesia (**fu ra n su** *ryō* **po ri ne shi a**)*

				領				

*Italic letters indicate the kanji pronunciation.

Answers

Commonly Mistaken Katakana (page 80) Part A 1. コ 2. ナ 3. ヌ 4. ス 5. ツ 6. ソ 7. テ 8. ウ
9. ク 10. ニ 11. ト 12. シ 13. チ 14. ケ 15. サ 16. カ 17. タ **Part B** 1. ノ 2. ム 3. リ 4. モ 5. ネ
6. ハ 7. ヨ 8. ロ 9. ヤ 10. メ 11. ヒ 12. ル 13. マ 14. ミ 15. ラ 16. フ 17. ユ

Commonly Mistaken Combined Characters (page 81) Part A 1. ギャ 2. シャ 3. ニョ 4. ミュ 5. ジョ 6. ピュ
7. キョ 8. チュ 9. ビャ 10. ヒャ 11. リョ 12. キャ 13. ビョ 14. ギョ 15. リュ **Part B** 1. ウィ 2. ドゥ 3. フォ
4. ヴォ 5. クォ 6. ヴァ 7. ティ 8. トゥ 9. ジェ 10. クァ 11. ヴェ 12. グァ 13. イェ 14. デュ 15. チェ

In My Home (page 82) Part A 1. ベッドルーム 2. シャワー 3. トイレ 4. リビングルーム 5. ダイニングルーム
6. キッチン **Part B** 2. ソファ、リビングルーム 3. スリッパ、トイレ 4. レンジ、キッチン 5. ミシン、クローゼット
6. スタンド、ベッドルーム 7. テーブル、ダイニングルーム 8. アイロン、クローゼット

Family Restaurant (Food, Part A) (page 83) メニュー 1. サンドイッチ 2. チーズピザ 3. ハンバーガ
ー 4. ホットドッグ 5. スパゲッティ 6. ラーメン 7. カレーライス 8. ハンバーグ 9. ステーキ 10. ポテトフライ
11. サラダ 12. スープ 13. クリームソーダ 14. トマトジュース 15. オレンジジュース 16. コーラ 17. ミルク
18. コーヒー 19. アイスティー 20. プリン 21. アイスクリーム 22. シャーベット 23. チーズケーキ

Picnic Lunch (Food, Part B) (page 84) 1. オレンジ 2. バナナ 3. メロン 4. パイナップル
5. マンゴー 6. キウイフルーツ 7. グレープフルーツ 8. チェリー 9. オリーブ 10. アボカド 11. トマト
12. レタス 13. セロリ 14. ピーナッツ 15. ポテトチップス 16. クッキー 17. クラッカー 18. キャンディー
19. チョコレート 20. ガム 21. アイスキャンディー 22. チーズ 23. ヨーグルト 24. ドレッシング 25. ケチャップ

Computers and Technology (page 85) 1. コンピューター 2. パソコン 3. ノートパソコン 4. マウス
5. キーボード 6. モニター 7. プリンター 8. ソフト 9. モデム 10. ウェブ 11. インターネット 12. ホームページ
13. メール 14. カメラ 15. デジカメ 16. ビデオカメラ 17. レンズ 18. フィルム 19. テレビ 20. リモコン
21. ビデオテープ 22. プレーヤー 23. プレーヤー 24. イヤホン 25. ラジオ 26. ケータイ

Sports and Athletics (page 86) 1. スポーツ 2. オリンピック 3. バスケットボール 4. バレーボール
5. ゴルフ 6. アメフト 7. ラクロス 8. テニス 9. ラグビー 10. サッカー 11. スコア 12. ゴール 13. チーム
14. ユニフォーム 15. スキー 16. スノーボード 17. アイススケート 18. アイスホッケー 19. サーフィン
20. ダイビング 21. スケボー 22. レスリング 23. ボクシング 24. テコンドー 25. マラソン

Sound Symbolic Words (page 87) 1. ザーザー 2. ヒューヒュー 3. リーン 4. チン 5. ワイワイ 6. ワンワン
7. ニャー 8. カーカー 9. ケロケロ 10. チューチュー 11. コケコッコー 12. ドキドキ 13. ワクワク

World Map: Africa (page 88) 1. アルジェリア 2. アンゴラ 3. ウガンダ 4. エジプト 5. エチオピア 6. エリトリア
7. ガーナ 8. カーボベルデ 9. カナリア 10. ガボン 11. カメルーン 12. ガンビア 13. ギニア 14. ギニアビサウ
15. コートジボワール 16. サントメプリンシペ 17. コンゴ 18. コンゴ 19. ケニア 20. コモロ 21. ザンビア
22. シエラレオネ 23. ジブチ 24. ジンバブエ 25. スーダン 26. スワジランド 27. セイシェル 28. ギニア
29. セネガル 30. ソマリア 31. タンザニア 32. チャド 33. チュニジア 34. トーゴ 35. ナイジェリア
36. ナミビア 37. ニジェール 38. アフリカ 39. サハラ 40. ブルキナファソ 41. ブルンジ 42. ベナン
43. ボツワナ 44. マダガスカル 45. マラウイ 46. マリ 47. モーリシャス 48. モーリタニア 49. モザンビーク
50. モロッコ 51. リビア 52. リベリア 53. ルワンダ 54. レソト 55. レユニオン 56. アフリカ

World Map: Asia and the Middle East (page 89) 1. キプロス 2. レバノン 3. パレスチナ 4. イスラエル 5. ヨルダン 6. モンゴル 7. マカオ 8. フィリピン 9. ベトナム 10. ラオス 11. カンボジア 12. ブルネイ 13. マレーシア 14. シンガポール 15. インドネシア 16. タイ 17. ミャンマー 18. バングラデシュ 19. ブータン 20. ネパール 21. インド 22. スリランカ 23. モルディヴ 24. パキスタン 25. アフガニスタン 26. イラン 27. タジキスタン 28. キルギス 29. カザフスタン 30. ウズベキスタン 31. トルクメニスタン 32. アゼルバイジャン 33. グルジア 34. トルコ 35. アルメニア 36. シリア 37. イラク 38. サウジアラビア 39. オマーン 40. イエメン 41. アラブ

World Map: Europe (page 90) 1. アイスランド 2. アイルランド 3. アルバニア 4. アンドラ 5. イギリス 6. イタリア 7. ウクライナ 8. エストニア 9. オーストリア 10. オランダ 11. ギリシャ 12. クロアチア 13. サンマリノ 14. ジブラルタル 15. スイス 16. スウェーデン 17. スペイン 18. スロバキア 19. スロベニア 20. チェコ 21. デンマーク 22. ドイツ 23. ノルウェー 24. バチカン 25. ハンガリー 26. フィンランド 27. フェロー 28. フランス 29. ロシア 30. ブルガリア 31. ベラルーシ 32. ベルギー 33. ポーランド 34. ポルトガル 35. マケドニア 36. マルタ 37. セルビア・モンテネグロ 38. モナコ 39. モルドバ 40. ラトビア 41. リトアニア 42. リヒテンシュタイン 43. ルーマニア 44. ルクセンブルク 45. ボスニア・ヘルツェゴビナ

World Map: North America and South America (page 91) 1. グリーンランド 2. カナダ 3. アメリカ 4. メキシコ 5. グアテマラ 6. ベリーズ 7. エルサルバドル 8. ホンジュラス 9. ニカラグア 10. コスタリカ 11. パナマ 12. バミューダ 13. バハマ 14. キューバ 15. ベネズエラ 16. コロンビア 17. エクアドル 18. ガイアナ 19. スリナム 20. フランス、ギアナ 21. ペルー 22. ブラジル 23. ボリビア 24. パラグアイ 25. チリ 26. アルゼンチン 27. ウルグアイ 28. フォークランド

World Map: Oceania (page 92) 1. アメリカ、サモア 2. オーストラリア 3. マリアナ 4. キリバス 5. グアム or グァム 6. クック 7. サモア 8. ソロモン 9. ツバル 10. トンガ 11. ナウル 12. ニューカレドニア 13. ニュージーランド 14. バヌアツ 15. パプアニューギニア 16. パラオ 17. フィジー 18. マーシャル 19. ミクロネシア 20. フランス、ポリネシア

FLASH CARDS

Suggested Activities

As mentioned in the Introduction it is much easier to learn to read katakana than to write it. With the right kinds of activities, diligent students can learn to read the basic 46 katakana in a few hours. You will more readily learn the writing once you have mastered katakana reading recognition, so it is suggested you begin with the flash cards at the end of the book.

Separate the flash cards by tearing or cutting along the perforated lines. If you are unfamiliar with katakana take the time to read the front and back of each flash card, paying close attention to the number and type of strokes used in each character. Many katakana characters look similar, and it is the number and type of strokes that will help to tell them apart.

Katakana Flash Card Drills (alone or with a partner): It is helpful to start with a few, perhaps 10, flash cards. You can test your reading recognition skills using the "smiley face" and "frowny face" diagrams below. Shuffle the flash cards and look at them one at a time. Say the name of the katakana character on the top flash card, then look at the back to see if you got it right. If so, place it on the "smiley face." If not, place it on the "frowny face." Continue looking at the flash cards one at a time and placing them in the appropriate pile. When you are finished, you will know which katakana characters you can read and which ones need more practice. Now put aside the ones you already know and study the flash cards you had difficulty with. When ready, repeat the activity with the difficult ones. As you gain mastery add more flash cards, until you know all 46! You can repeat this simple activity from time to time to refresh your basic katakana reading skills.

Katakana Chart Activity (alone or with a small group): This is an excellent activity to improve your katakana recognition skills and become familiar with **gojūon** order—the way dictionaries, web searches, etc, are organized. Place all the flash cards on a large surface (i.e. the floor) face up, in random order. Then, try to put them into order as quickly as possible. For an extra challenge use a stopwatch.

Katakana Pick-up (small group): Place all the flash cards on a large surface face up, in order or mixed up. One person calls the name of a katakana character and the other players try to quickly put their hand on it. The first one gets to keep it. Continue playing, and when all the flash cards are gone, count to see who has the most. The winner gets to be the "caller" for the next game!

Acknowledgements

I am grateful to many individuals who have contributed valuable comments and suggestions. I wish to thank my former colleagues at the American School in Japan: Keiko Yasuno, Keiko Ando, Sumino Hirano, Mariko Smisson, Yuko Hayashi, and Clark Tenney. I also wish to thank Noriko Okada (Waterford School) and Shauna Stout for their careful proofreading and valuable feedback. I express my gratitude to the helpful people at Tuttle Publishing.

ア	イ	ウ
エ	オ	カ
キ	ク	ケ
コ	サ	シ

3 "u" as in y**ou**

"**Oo**oo!" The water balloon was cold as it splashed on his back!

2 "i" as in **ea**sy

An **ea**sel holds your picture while you work on it or display it.

1 "a" as in f**a**ther

"**A**AAaaa!" cried the critter as he fell off the edge of the cliff.

6 "ka" as in **ca**r

Katakana "**ka**" カ and hiragana "**ka**" か look a bit alike.

5 "o" as in **oa**k

an **O**lympic figure skater

4 "e" as in r**e**d

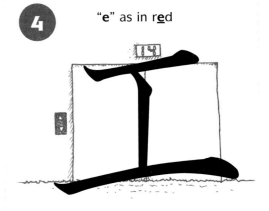

elevator doors

9 "ke" as in **Ke**vin

a **ka**ngaroo

8 "ku" as in cuc**koo**

a **cool** way to write seven (7)

7 "ki" as in **key**

Katakana "**ki**" キ and hiragana "**ki**" き look a bit alike.

12 "shi" as in **she**

She tilted her head and smiled.

11 "sa" as in **sa**w

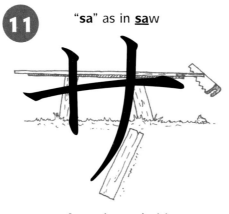

A **saw**horse holds wood while you cut it.

10 "ko" as in **co**coa

a cup of hot **co**coa

ス	セ	ソ
タ	チ	ツ
テ	ト	ナ
ニ	ヌ	ネ

15 "so" as in <u>so</u>

When other kid said, "You only have one eye," he said, "<u>So</u>!"

14 "se" as in <u>se</u>t

Katakana "se" and hiragana "se" look a little alike.

13 "su" as in <u>su</u>per

It's <u>Su</u>perman, er super-critter.

18 "tsu" as in ca<u>ts</u>

<u>Two</u> children are sliding down a slide. ("ts" like ca<u>ts</u> and "u" like y<u>ou</u>)

17 "chi" as in <u>chee</u>r

a <u>chee</u>rleader

16 "ta" as in t<u>a</u>ll

the leaning <u>to</u>wer of Pisa (In Japanese "tower" is pronounced with a "ta" as in t<u>a</u>ll).

21 "na" as in <u>no</u>t

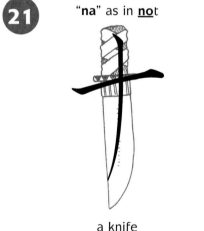

a knife

20 "to" as in <u>to</u>tem

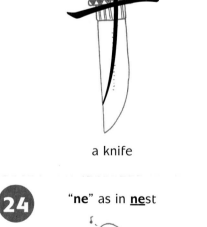

a <u>to</u>tem pole

19 "te" as in <u>te</u>lephone

a <u>te</u>lephone pole and wires

24 "ne" as in <u>ne</u>st

a <u>ne</u>st on top of a tree

23 "nu" as in <u>new</u>

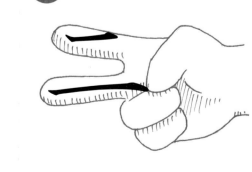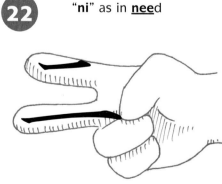

a <u>new</u> way to write seven (7)

22 "ni" as in <u>nee</u>d

The Japanese word for "two" is <u>ni</u>.

ノ	ハ	ヒ
フ	ヘ	ホ
マ	ミ	ム
メ	モ	ヤ

27 "**hi**" as in **he**

He drives the car.

26 "**ha**" as in **ha**wk

the two wings of a fearsome **ha**wk (or a slightly dazed looking hawk)

25 "**no**" as in **no**se

a **no**se

30 "**ho**" as in **Ho**! **Ho**!

Mr. "**Ho Ho**" laughs even when stuck in a chimney!

29 "**he**" as in **he**lp

No significant differences between katakana "**he**" and hiragana "**he**."

28 "**fu**" as in **Hoot!**

The owl cries, "**Hoot**! **Hoot**!" (Pronounce "**fu**" without touching the upper teeth and lower lip).

33 "**mu**" as in **moo**

I love ja**mu** (jam)!

32 "**mi**" as in **me**ow

A cat's three whiskers, "**Me**ow!"

31 "**ma**" as in **mo**m

Mom holds Baby while she attends to some work.

36 "**ya**" as in **ya**rn

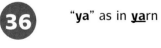

Hiragana "*ya*" and katakana "*ya*" look a bit alike.

35 "**mo**" as in **mo**re

Hiragana "*mo*" and katakana "*mo*" look a bit alike.

34 "**me**" as in **Me**xico

the "X" in **Me**xico